THE
PERFECT HOME

THE
PERFECT HOME

Mary Gilliatt

PORTLAND HOUSE
NEW YORK

For my patient and dear mother

Riviera Villa

This splendid neo-Palladian house (*right and preceding pages*), with its magnificent garden vistas, as well as spectacular views over the Mediterranean and the mountains, epitomizes the luxury and style of the French Riviera. It is hardly surprising, then, to discover that it was used as one of the settings for Alfred Hitchcock's movie, *To Catch A Thief*. But the most interesting thing about the house is that until it was transformed by the owner, with American designer Thomas Brookes Kyle, it was a dull, Florentine-style villa dating from 1910 and had no garden at all.

Mr Kyle completely gutted it, re-ordered the interiors, bought magnificent eighteenth-century French and English furniture and Russian chandeliers, and laid out the lavish grounds, planting the now mature cypresses, eucalyptus, pines and sycamores, as well as building pools and fountains, terraces and balustrades – a revival that captures the essential glamour of the Riviera.

First published in 1987 as *Dream Houses* by
Conran Octopus Limited, 37 Shelton Street, London WC2H 9HN

Copyright © 1987 Mary Gilliatt

This 1991 edition published by Portland House, distributed by Outlet Book Company Inc., a Random House Company, 225 Park Avenue South, New York, New York 10003.

Printed and bound in Hong Kong
ISBN 0-517-05181-8
87654321

Contents

THE ROMANTIC IDEAL

THE PAST RELIVED

THE PERSONAL VISION

THE SPIRIT OF PLACE

*I*ntroduction

The German writer, Goethe, poet, philosopher and Romantic, was entirely practical when it came to houses. 'Three things', he said, 'are to be looked for in a building. That it stand on the right spot; that it be securely founded; that it be successfully executed.' All this is undoubtedly true. But for many people there is a fourth, more intangible requirement, rarely articulated, let alone achieved, but which almost always exists in the mind of a potential buyer or builder. This is that the house (or apartment) should fulfil a dream.

Almost everyone has some sort of dream or ideal, however illogical, impractical or grandiose, of the kind of home they would like to own, and where it should be. It might be a romantic, nostalgic dream, based on childhood memories, half-forgotten and hazy, not necessarily architectural at all, which merge with remembered feelings and scents. The sun shafting across a brick-floored country hall; a small square window framing a blue-green wedge of sky and sea; jasmine climbing up the pillars of a porch; French windows flung open onto a lavender-edged terrace; the smell of fresh mown grass on a summer morning; or woodsmoke drifting in the sharp evening air – any of these fragments might vividly evoke a loved house just as the taste of *madeleine* cake inspired memories for Proust. But the dream need not be nostalgic; it may simply be the memory of a coveted house or piece of land, which may lead to the ambition to own a similar house in similar surroundings one day.

Happily for today's dreamers, there have always been people who build for love, for delight, for dalliance, or as a memorial to days of glory, with the hope of resuscitating the

Above: *The fourteenth-century Moorish palace, the Alhambra, is a memorial to a lost empire.*
Right: *The Lake Palace at Udaipur in India dates from the eighteenth century.*

pleasure. This has never changed. And the inheritors, the restorers, the preservers, the buyers who come for generations, even for centuries, after these original builders, are very conscious of their prizes. Many people dream of the chance to revive such a building, to restore it tenderly and sensitively to life. Or their pleasure is to recreate or reinterpret an ancient ideal and build a modern classic, complete in every detail; or to transpose a model from another century into the context of the present time.

Occasionally there is true personal vision, a sense of mission, someone imbued with 'the superior passion for building', as the early twentieth-century German architectural writer, Paul Scheerbart, put it, 'which ought to be the cooperative effort of many enthusiastic people who out of their love for the world, add something new to it, something great and splendid, a work which towers far above the individual...' The period following the devastation of World War I was full of such enthusiasm and idealism. Interestingly, the young Walter Gropius, a founder of the Bauhaus, also wrote in 1919: 'Ideas perish as soon as they are compromised. Therefore distinguish clearly between dream and reality, between everyday work and a longing for the stars ... go into the buildings ... engrave your ideas on their naked walls – and build in fantasy without regard for technical difficulties. To have the gift of imagination is more important than all technology, which always adapts itself to man's creative will...' Such grand words, such emotion, but there have always been people with just such a passion for building, an *idée fixe*, a *beau idéal*, even an obsession, determined to fulfil their fantasies or their follies.

Again there are people imbued with the spirit of a particular place. They want, *need*, to live on the top of a mountain, or perched on a cliff, or right by the sea, on a tropical beach, or to make a floating home on a river. They will give up many normal conveniences for the chance of living in the middle of water meadows, or to restore a ravaged landscape to beauty. 'We are the children of our landscape,' wrote Lawrence Durrell in *The Alexandrian Quartet*. 'It dictates behaviour and even thought in the measure to which we are responsive to it.'

All through history and all over the world, such dreams have resulted in great buildings. The Moorish style of the fourteenth century is responsible for some of the most intricate architectural fantasies that exist. The exquisite Alhambra Palace in Granada, with its languorous, softly acqueous atmosphere, gilded honeycomb ceilings, Koranic descriptions of Paradise on the walls and pavilions which seem to float on water, is a swansong to Muslim Spain. Built by the Nasud dynasty as a beautiful refuge and escape from the harsh reality of losing their pre-eminence, it seems both sweet and sad, sumptuous yet insubstantial. It could hardly be a more enduring memorial to a lost empire.

The Indian Taj Mahal in Agra is another great memorial, not so much to nostalgia as to enduring love. Its white marble, incised with such precision and beauty, reflects every nuance of light, hazy with soft violet and rose at dawn, dazzling at midday, glowing in the sunset. Shah Jahan, the Moghul Emperor, heartbroken at the death of his wife, Mumtaz, after seventeen blissful years of marriage, started to build the Taj as a memorial to her in 1631. The building took 20,000 labourers and craftsman twenty-one years to complete.

Another famous white marble Indian palace was built around a century later in the middle of the Pichola Lake at Udaipur, but this time as a summer retreat for the maharana and his many ladies. Courtyards inset with lotus pools and bougainvillaea, and terraces overgrown with jasmine were surrounded by rooms decorated with crystal, silks, and wall paintings of dancing girls and hunting scenes. Known simply as the Lake Palace, it is an idyllic place, built solely for pleasure.

In France, at much the same time, Madame de Pompadour, mistress of Louis XV, was creating the elegant little 'love nests' which she had built to welcome the king, who, in his turn, was one of the world's great builders. He was only really happy, Madame de Pompadour is reported to have said, when he had a heap of architectural designs spread before him. Madame de Pompadour died before the neo-classical Petit Trianon at Versailles, designed by the court architect, Gabriel, was completed, but it remains an exquisite little monument to love.

The Petit Trianon could hardly be more different in feeling and scale to the Royal Pavilion at Brighton, another of the great exotic buildings dedicated to the fulfilment of pleasure. Looking now at this stuccoed neo-Moghul extravaganza, one can barely imagine the vicissitudes of its construction – which were far from dream-like. In 1781, the extravagant, fashionable Prince Regent, fresh from his Chinoiserie triumph at his home, Carlton House in London, and his secret marriage to Mrs Fitzherbert, decided to buy a

Opposite left: *Vanbrugh's triumph, Castle Howard.* Opposite right: *A monument to love, the Petit Trianon at Versailles.* Below: *Thomas Jefferson's home, Monticello.*

house in Brighton, of which he had grown rather fond. Brighton also attracted the prince because it was far enough away from his father to enable him to live more openly with his beloved. He bought a fairly ordinary farmhouse and commissioned the architect Henry Holland to transform it into a marine pavilion. The result, though pleasant and in the classic style, rapidly proved to be inadequate for the royal tastes, and in 1802 enlargements were started with the idea of clothing the building 'in Chinese garb'.

A year later, Mr Holland's team were summarily succeeded by William Porden who set about plans for a new pavilion to be built all in Chinoiserie. However, Porden began with the royal stables, riding school and coach house, using the newly fashionable Indian style, based on paintings and engravings of buildings in Agra and Delhi brought back by those English travellers and artists, William Hodges and Thomas and William Daniell. That the stables were started first was not so surprising. Continental visitors were apt to remark, or grumble, that the English lavished more attention on their horses than their houses. While the stables were still being built in all their Eastern glory, the prince, who it seems was as profligate with his architects as Henry VIII was with his wives, asked another distinguished architect of the time, Humphrey Repton, to come and give *his* opinion of the best style for the projected pavilions.

Repton's reply is worth repeating as much for its run-through of eclectic architectural

Above left: *The London townhouse of Sir John Soane is an architectural landmark.* Above right: *The ultimate vision of grandeur, Neuschwanstein Castle in Bavaria.*

styles as for its ponderous language, so much at odds (as so many architects' writings) with the eventual building: 'I could not hesitate in agreeing', he wrote, 'that neither the Grecian nor the Gothic style could be made to assimilate with what had so much the character of an Eastern building. The Turkish was objectionable as being a corruption of the Grecian; the Moorish as a bad model of the Gothic; the Egyptian as too ambitious for the character of the villa; the Chinese too light and drifting for the outside however it might be applied to the interior. Thus if any house style were to be adopted, no alternative remained but to combine from the architecture of Hinduism such forms as might be applicable to the purpose.'

Repton's 1806 plans for a Hindu pleasure dome were considered 'delightful' by the prince but, alas, the coffers were going through a lean time and the plans were shelved. However, the design was not forgotten. In 1815, much to Repton's fury, the prince commissioned John Nash to execute the designs in the style we see now. In all, the dream took some thirty-four years from its original conception.

Two very disparate, beautiful houses, continents apart, were built by distinguished men who were not primarily architects. Castle Howard in Yorkshire, with its great domes, cupolas, urns and statues, was called 'one of the most thrilling experiences in English architecture' by Gervase Jackson-Stops in his *English Country Houses – A Grand Tour*. It was

Above: *Brighton Pavilion was a dream that was thirty-four years in the making. It was conceived as a pleasure palace by the Prince Regent, later George IV.*

Sir John Vanbrugh's ideal of a great house, all the more remarkable for the fact that Vanbrugh was first a soldier, then a playwright. It was therefore totally surprising that he was chosen by the Earl of Carlisle in 1699 to draw up designs for the great mansion the earl was proposing to build on his Yorkshire estate. As Jonathan Swift wrote bitingly:

Van's genius without thought or lecture,
Is hugely turned to architecture.

But Vanbrugh, greatly helped by Nicholas Hawksmoor as draughtsman and clerk of works, confounded Swift to design some of the greatest and most original of British houses. 'I have seen gigantic palaces before', wrote Sir Horace Walpole after a visit to Castle Howard, 'but never a sublime one.'

Like Vanbrugh, Thomas Jefferson, one of America's great early presidents and statesmen, was also a man of many talents and sensibilities, and not least, a great neo-classical designer, as his buildings for the University of Virginia show. He built his own elegant, enduring house, Monticello, in the same state, to incorporate his many original ideas and inventions, and saw the house through to the last decorational detail, even to the window treatments. In fact his designs for pelmets – 'Drapery for the tops of four windows ... no curtains being desired' – resulted in the festooned pelmets without curtains or draperies so popular for colonial houses all over America today. Indeed, since the house and gardens have long been open to the public in their original, but carefully nurtured state, they have inspired very much more than window treatments.

Sir John Soane, who died in 1837, the year Queen Victoria came to the throne, was the last of the great Georgian neo-classicists and willed that his London townhouse with all its contents become a museum after his death. Like Thomas Jefferson, Soane had poured all his talents, genius and ideas into his own house, experimenting with spatial vistas and lighting in what are actually diminutive rooms.

Painters and architects, who need to be professional dreamers, are often at their creative best in their own houses, when it is not a question of money but of spirit. Monet's country house at Giverny, near Paris, is as much a source of inspiration in its simple way as Soane's sophisticated London terrace. Its vibrant blue and yellow colour schemes set

Top left: *Monet's home, Giverny.* Left: *The sweeping organic style of the Spanish architect, Antonio Gaudí.* Below left and right: *William Randolph Hearst's mansion, San Simeon.*

against the soft splendours of the garden outside remain full of vitality even today.

But what about the grandiose dreams that are obsessive enough to bring more pain than pleasure, or even to bring ruin? There is the historic case of Louis XIV's Finance Minister, Nicholas Le Fouquet, who was ambitious enough, and foolish enough, to build the oversumptuous Vaux le Vicomte, a house that tried to outshine the king's. Not only was it rushed up too quickly in time for a *grande fête* to which all the court of Fontainebleau were invited, but it not unnaturally displeased the monarch who was not known as *le Roi Soleil* for nothing. No sun likes to be outshined. Le Fouquet's downfall was arranged.

Ludwig, the Mad King of Bavaria, was also carried away by dreams of grandeur, not so much in order to outshine all competition, but because he was hopelessly extravagant in his architectural ambitions. And, on a scale that could rival the achievements of a Great Gatsby, there was also the amazing mansion built by William Randolph Hearst, San Simeon: a true *folie de grandeur*.

In the late nineteenth and the early twentieth century, there was an obsession with organic forms in buildings. The two leading exponents of this were the Spanish Antonio Gaudí and the American Frank Lloyd Wright. Gaudí began by being an academic well acquainted with historic styles, including, like the present-day Ricardo Bofill, the indigenous styles of his own region. But in the 1890s, he abandoned these influences, and

Above: *Falling Water by Frank Lloyd Wright, built for Edgar J. Kauffman in 1936–38.*

his work began to reflect an interest in nature, or 'God's architecture' as he called it, using forms that had seldom been used in architecture before.

Frank Lloyd Wright, one of the early founders of modern architecture, adhered to a different sort of organic approach. He liked his houses to fuse thoroughly with their site, for the inside to become part of the outside. In one of the great dream houses of modern times, Falling Water, the house he built for Edgar J. Kauffman between 1936 and 1938, a series of free-floating platforms were balanced audaciously over a small waterfall, and anchored to the natural rock. Inside there are rough stone walls and flagged floors to continue the elemental ruggedness.

Of all the dream houses, or houses that are considered architectural dreams, to be built in this century, and of all the fantasy architecture that exists, probably the most revolutionary houses have been those made of glass. Philip Johnson built his classic glass house in New Canaan in 1955–6, a building that epitomizes the modern age, with its audacious technology.

If we can learn anything from the houses in this book and their stories, it must be that this determination to make dreams reality might be the most practical quality of all. Irrational and defiant, it is a spirit that overcomes technical problems, a personal sense of mission that can achieve the impossible.

Above: *Philip Johnson's glass house in New Canaan, a dream of technology.*

THE ROMANTIC IDEAL

There's a fascination frantic
In a ruin that's romantic

W. S. GILBERT

Glenveagh Castle

Glenveagh Castle, in County Donegal, is one of those vast Victorian piles built in the early 1870s at a time of high prosperity. Situated in what must be one of the most beautiful wild landscapes in Ireland, which is, after all, a country full of wild grandeur, it stands on a slight promontory jutting into Loch Veagh. Yet, despite the very Irishness of its setting, three of the past owners of Glenveagh have been Americans.

Glenveagh was originally designed as a four-storey rectangular keep by John Townsend Trench in 1870–73 for his cousin, the infamous John Adair, whose terrible reputation throughout Ireland was the result of his eviction of 254 tenants in the miserable cold April of 1861. The round tower was apparently an afterthought.

Adair's wife, married long after the eviction incident, was a wealthy American widow. Cornelia Ritchie (formerly Wadsworth) was a kind and generous woman who seems to have been just as much a contrast to her husband as the luxuriant and rare flora she planted were to the rugged granite masses of the castle walls.

Adair died in 1885. His wife lived on in Glenveagh until 1921, perfecting her gardens, planting more and more rare and exotic botanical specimens from as far afield as Chile and Tasmania, and entertaining in the grand tradition of American hostesses of that era. Edward VII sent her a stag from Windsor Castle to help start the herd of deer which now, a century or so later, has expanded to nearly a thousand. Just as the deer thrived and expanded so have the gardens, and in June the air is full of a quite extraordinary fragrance from the rhododendrons and the azaleas.

After Mrs Adair's death, the castle was occupied by the IRA for a time, but they evacuated quickly when the Free State Army approached. Then Glenveagh was used by the army as a garrison for three years.

It was the task of another American, Professor Arthur Kingsley Porter, a distinguished archeologist and Profesor of Fine Arts at Harvard, to halt Glenveagh's decline. He renovated and repaired the property, mended the deer fence and tended both castle and grounds with care until his tragic death – ironically, he drowned in a loch.

In 1938 Glenveagh was bought by its third American proprietor, Mr Henry McIlhenny of Philadelphia, who was for thirty years Curator of Decorative Arts at the Philadelphia Museum where he subsequently became

Above and right: Exquisitely planned gardens and rare botanical specimens soften and domesticate the grey mass of the castle walls.

Vice-President. Since Mr McIlhenny's grandfather was born in Ireland, it was a home-coming of a sort.

Mr McIlhenny had a fine reputation for creating glorious houses and an equally fine reputation as a host. He continued to tend and nurture both castle and exotic gardens, turning the interior into one of the most comfortable, civilized and idiosyncratic of houses, in splendid juxtaposition to the austere mountains which surround it, and the great grey expanse of the loch.

The rounded windows with their plate glass and polished brass fittings, the blazing turf fires in every grate to counteract the well-known Irish damp, the Victorian paintings by Landseer, Ansdell, Buckner and A.E. (George Russell), the rich clear colours, the handsome eighteenth-century Irish furniture mixed with the odd piece of high Victoriana, quite apart from the legendary McIlhenny hospitality, made any visit to Glenveagh an extraordinarily nostalgic experience which is still recalled by many.

The entrance hall with its *coquillage* decoration of sea shells embedded in plaster was punctuated by antlers every few yards, felled progeny of that original Edwardian stag. The Red Sitting Room, with its long white sofa (with splendidly practical 'mall' drinks tables from Hong Kong embedded in its upholstered arms), its lion and unicorn mirror and its white red-bordered curtains, was a particularly good nineteenth-century room.

The drawing room was really a grand salon with its delicate Georgian furniture, its French chintz and its rugs woven specially in Portugal to match the fabric. In contrast, the Music Room had a gloriously Victorian flavour with spectacular antler candelabra. Bathrooms were solidly luxurious in the best American manner.

Outside, all the outbuildings were grandly castellated, and Mr McIlhenny had all the woodwork painted a Tuscan green, his estate colour. He even improved on Mrs Adair's garden designs by adding a sweet-smelling rose garden, a wild garden, and a flight of one hundred steps leading up to a hillside vantage point.

The legendary days are over. In 1981, Henry McIlhenny presented Glenveagh Castle and its gardens to the Irish nation, having already sold the lands to the Irish National Parks and Monuments Service in 1975. But many of the rooms still have their original furnishings and decorations and the whole is both a spectacular reminder of bygone glories, and continuing proof of that affection many Americans feel for the 'old country'.

Opposite top left: *The hall.* Opposite top right: *The Music Room.* Left: *The drawing room.*
Top: *Bathroom in the American tradition.* Above: *Loch Veagh.*

Liselund

Liselund in Denmark, a perfectly preserved neo-classical rustic building, is one of the happiest of houses as well as one of the most harmonious. It was built in the late eighteenth century by Baron Antoine de la Calmette as a love-token for his wife, Elisabeth, whom he called Lisa.

The Baron, son of the Dutch Ambassador to the Throne of Denmark and himself a Gentleman of the Royal Bedchamber, was a man of great sophistication and taste. In 1783 he bought the little manor of Somarkegaard on Moen Island only twelve miles (20 km) from his home, Marienborg. To the Baron, Somarkegaard seemed unique in that it managed to present on one estate many of the attributes that the new feeling for nature demanded, including dramatic chalk cliffs and thick beech forests set against the background of the sea.

It was a perfect place, in fact, to create a version of the English parks so lately fashionable throughout Europe, and to take advantage of the Rousseau-esque ideals of the time, when the adoration of nature and the simple life was embraced with heartfelt enthusiasm by the rich. Such estates included skilful water effects, classical allusions, oriental edifices, chasms, waterfalls, wildernesses, hermits' huts and other follies – 'nature' punctuated with diversions from other cultures.

De la Calmette began his venture by renaming his new property Liselund – Lisa's Wood – after his wife,

and then spent eight years developing the park, digging and landscaping drainage ditches to resemble a winding river, creating islands, dells, waterfalls, and the requisite chasm, planting exotica and importing wildfowl. He also built a Chinese pagoda to use as a tea parlour; a rugged Norwegian cabin to mark the beginning of the forest path leading down the white chalk cliffs to the sea; a Gothic ruin, placed by the chasm to remind light-hearted visitors of their mortality; and a nostalgic gardener's cottage tucked into a hillside, its facade wrapped in logs and its roof thatched to resemble a Swiss chalet.

To this woodland idyll the de la Calmettes brought guests to picnic, botanize, wander and generally dilly-dally. They always returned to Marienborg at night, for Liselund still lacked a residence proper.

Finally, in 1792, the Baron began construction of his little summer palace. Andreas Kirkerup, who was court architect at the time as well as a popular designer of graceful country houses, was briefed with sketches the Baron had made in France. But Kirkerup was an ardent classicist and one of his first plans, which featured the thatched roof demanded by the de la Calmettes to emphasize the rusticity of the site, but set over a Greek-pillared classical facade, was a comic disaster.

Undeterred, the Baron persevered in his quest for perfect simplicity and perfect symmetry, and the final design is a dream that matches the idyllic setting. Built

Left: *Liselund seen across the small lake.* Above: *Detail of the roof. Antoine de la Calmette insisted on thatching to give the house a rural charm.*

in the form of a 'T', with the broad front as the main facade, Kirkerup's Greek columns are reduced to four simple wooden pillars or abacuses, carrying the projection of the roof above a flight of wide steps and framing the entrance of three French doors. The dining-room wing is also guarded by a simple peristyle of wooden columns. A little spire with a bell and a weathercock, plaster garlands under the side windows, whitewashed brick walls and delicately formed lamps on stone pedestals complete the exterior detailing.

Inside, the most elaborate room is the dining room, for the house, after all, was principally built for entertaining. It takes up the entire back wing of the building and is a masterpiece of decorative painting. All the classical architectural details are actually clever *trompe l'oeil*, for the panels and grey mouldings outlining the windows and mirrors are painted *faux marbre*. The deal floor is also painted to resemble black and white marble tiles, and even the chairs are painted, though they look carved with pastel tendrils and rope-like curves. Only a little gilding on the frames of the mirrors and the blue glass in the prisms of the chandeliers break up the predominant black, grey and white, with these small elements of colour standing out brilliantly against the calm restraint of the rest.

The three glass doors of the main entrance open into a large square room, which is both entrance hall and garden room, done in a simplified Louis XVI style. Sofas and chairs are lined up against the wainscoting in the approved arrangement of the time, and the corners of the room are splayed and provided with domed niches which hold altar-like constructions. One of these is actually a stove made of steatite on a base of Norwegian marble. The other is a simple cabinet of marbled wood which provides the symmetry always present at Liselund.

To the right of the Garden Room is the Monkey Room, named after the monkey painted on the pier glass set in the central panel on the back wall. The monkey in question is a life-sized portrait of an old family pet, honoured because he had saved the Baron's father from being burned to death when he was ambassador in Lisbon. The household was asleep when the flames started and the animal's screeching woke everyone up in time to evacuate the house. From his painted perch, the animal reaches into the fronds of one of four magnificently sculpted palm trees. These form the frame of both the pier glass and one of the most striking

Right: *The dining room is a masterpiece of* trompe l'oeil. *The details and floor tiles are painted.*

illusions in this house of *trompe l'oeil*, a scene showing the embassy garden in Lisbon viewed through a bamboo lattice painted in yellow. Facing the monkey tribute are twin oval mirrors, two of several such graceful mirrors around the house, complete with corbels and antique decorations, which match the Wedgwood-style medallions on the remaining walls. In each corner at the back of the room are Etruscan iron urns, one of which is actually a disguised stove.

On the other side of the Garden Room is the Baroness's bedroom. This displays much the same proportions but a much greater simplicity. A built-in closet in each rear corner makes a niche for a canopied bed. One closet conceals a commode, the other a passageway to the Baron's bedroom, and both closet doors are painted with *trompe l'oeil torchères* holding flower arrangements. The simple canopy over the bed is made of fine linen huckaback and the floor is left bare once again to emphasize the rurality of the place.

Charming as it was, and expensive as it was to create, Liselund was never anything more than a summer house. With only eleven bedrooms it was too small for the de la Calmette household, and was only used for the few weeks in the year when the family were prepared to camp out. Liselund became a home for the first time when the Baron's heir, Charles, married a commoner, much against his parents' wishes, and brought his wife to live here. Although Charles inherited the entire estate at the beginning of the nineteenth century, he lacked his parents' talents and died bankrupt in 1820 at forty.

Liselund was bought by the Rosenkrantz family who permitted Charles's wife to stay on at the house for the next fifty-seven years of her widowhood. 'Aunt Calmette', as she was called, never allowed the furniture to be rearranged or a detail to be altered, and insisted on maintaining the property exactly how her husband had left it. She had a great fondness for white and kept only white creatures around her: white poultry, peahens, and an albino roe which followed her everywhere.

When Aunt Calmette died in 1877 she left a perfectly preserved eighteenth-century *petit palais*. The Rosenkrantz family used it for only ten years, then moved to a new house they had constructed discreetly elsewhere on the estate. Today, the present Baron Rosenkrantz heads the board of directors that continues to maintain Liselund as the treasure it is.

Above left and right: *The Monkey Room with its splendid decorations and* trompe l'oeil. Right:
The simplicity of the Baroness's bedroom emphasizes the rustic setting.

*N*indooinbah *H*ouse

Nindooinbah House at Beaudesert, South Queensland is considered to be one of the most beautiful and most typical of Queensland's old homesteads with its stilt construction, elegant low-lying symmetry and generous verandah space. Built in the 1840s and sensitively extended and renovated in 1906 by the then leading Australian architect, Robin Dods, it stands in 480 acres (194 hectares) of farm and grazing land intercepted by the Albert River, sprawling languidly under the intense Australian sun.

The result of Dods' turn-of-the-century conversion is a U-shaped building, mostly only one room's breadth wide, perfectly designed for the climate. Pairs of French windows set opposite each other provide continual cross-breezes, wafting in scents from the garden which sweeps down to a lagoon. Access to any particular room is either from the verandah or from the room adjoining.

Dods played a few tricks with perspective. The house is not perfectly symmetrical, although it appears to be so. The verandahs narrow appreciably in places, yet the illusion is created that they are equally wide all the way around the house.

But there is something more to Nindooinbah than

Left: *Nindooinbah, low-lying against the palm trees is a perfect example of an early Queensland homestead.* Above: *An old-fashioned flower garden to the front of the house.*

apposite architecture, a romantic garden and estate dotted with palms. It has been inhabited by the same family for three generations, all of whom have added possessions and character, so it has about it the sort of atmosphere that only a house continually lived in by one family can have, a sort of impregnation of spirit and continuity, the calm of a much-loved and rooted space. It is also possessed of a good many near-perfect Edwardian interiors.

Margaret de Burgh Persse, now married to painter Patrick Hockey, inherited the house and, together with her husband, has restored it to its original grandeur. Nindooinbah was bought in 1906 for her grandfather, William Collins, by the family company, John Collins and Sons, which for many years had been renting the property, then encompassing about 20,000 acres (8,000 hectares). Collins had been using the place as a cattle-fattening farm in conjunction with other extensive holdings locally and in Western Queensland and the Northern Territory.

William Collins was the first white child to be born in the area, which was otherwise populated by aborigines. He was a man who grew to enjoy a certain style and, when Nindooinbah was bought for him six years after his rather late marriage, he clearly decided to impress Gwendoline, his young bride, with the extensions, enlargements and splendid furnishings.

Some years later, in 1920, the house saw another alteration – when Mrs Collins converted the entrance porch to make a ballroom in order to give a dance for the visit of the Prince of Wales, later to become Edward VIII. Alas, the prince did not feel like going out that night and chose not to come. Mrs William Collins, by all accounts, was not best pleased.

Life was conducted in a rather formal style at the homestead, with a very large staff in attendance, and the family eating night after night in the dining room with all the silver laid out. The present generation, however, have broken this tradition and almost always eat out on the verandah, moving from one point to another according to the position of the sun. And after sunset, the sweet scent of the honeysuckle and quisqualis is intoxicating in the balmy night air with not another light to be seen in the velvety blackness.

In some ways, the actual furnishings of the house are reminiscent of a prosperous tea-planter's house in Darjeeling. Much of the furniture was bought in Japan and Europe during the Collins' honeymoon in 1900 and, although distinctly Edwardian, the house has the Eastern air fashionable at the time. It is a remarkable

Top left: *The formal dining room, dating from 1906.* Top right: *A guest bedroom.* Opposite: *Perfect Edwardiana in the drawing room. Original lace blinds, dating from 1908, were restored.*

repository of household and personal items from the whole of the twentieth century, with perfectly preserved furnishings, china, even clothes. The court dress worn by Gwendoline Collins when she was presented at Buckingham Palace, still hangs resplendently in a wardrobe, its original jet and crystal beads intact. And linen sheets bought over fifty years ago in London still lie, beautifully tissued, in their original boxes, as do wedding presents sent to Margaret Hockey's mother, Mrs Robert Persse: Lalique bowls, elaborate dinner services, exquisite linens, a plethora of expensive household goods that simply were not needed in a house already amply stocked.

Given this status quo, it would be difficult to make any radical changes and certainly the Hockeys are not about to do so. A lick of paint there, a bit of rearrangement here, but no real changes of colour or replenishments. The Hockeys feel very strongly that it is important to preserve the feel of the house, to keep 'all the mish-mash of belongings that you get with time'. All they have really done, they say, is work on the garden and move things around a little in the house.

Some restoration work did need to be done. Fine lace blinds in the drawing room were patiently mended by a friend as a wedding present to the Hockeys. The work took eighty hours.

All the Edwardian splendour remains, making a staid and strait-laced contrast to the golden scene outside. The dining room with its silky oak panelling and walls of long windows was an integral part of Robin Dods' 1906 extension. Interestingly, the elaborate plaster ceiling was executed by Mrs Dods, who was a plasterer, an unusual feminine occupation, especially in the early part of the century.

The drawing room is another room of regal Edwardiana, with a deep and elaborately hand-painted frieze and a cedar mantelpiece and cupboards. Again, the furniture dates back to Dods' renovation.

The guest room in the bedroom extension has cedar mouldings and another hand-painted frieze of lotus flowers. All the furniture is made from a bunya pine that Dods had to have chopped down in order to build the new wing. William Collins, apparently, was so distressed at the loss of the tree, that Dods had to placate him by recycling it into furniture for the space.

The famous ballroom *cum* entrance hall, added on so proudly for the Prince of Wales's visit and so carelessly rejected, is still used for dances, although normally the high-pitched room is filled with chintz and rattan and massed with flowers from the garden. There are still saddles and bridles on a stand from the Persses' days, along with various sporting trophies.

With the Hockeys' marriage, cattle from Patrick Hockey's own estate now come to Nindooinbah to fatten. And paintings by Patrick Hockey can be found on the walls in some of the rooms. Appropriately enough, they depict flowers and, in one case, a Nindooinbah interior view.

The only really major change in lifestyle for this current generation is that they live so much more of their lives out on the verandah. Times change, even if the house does not, and casual rather than formal is now the fashion. And who could disagree, with all that golden light and sweet-smelling air to be enjoyed at every possible opportunity.

The large staff, too, has diminished, but a couple of second-generation employees are still part of the household, and there are grandchildren of former employees working there now. It is that sort of place; familial, comforting, easeful. Whoever you are, once you have spent any sort of time there, you get to feel you belong to the house.

Opposite top left: *The much-used verandah, now a place for dining and general relaxation.*
Opposite top right: *The nursery verandah.* Left: *The ballroom was converted from the entrance hall in 1920 by Mrs William Collins in anticipation of a visit from the then Prince of Wales.* Above: *The view from the verandah at Nindooinbah House.*

T_{he} C_{onvent}

This curiously pinnacled and thatched folly, looking like a Gothic version of Hansel and Gretel's gingerbread house, was built by Henry Hoare the Younger as part of his remarkable eighteenth-century estate, Stourhead, in Wiltshire, one of the greatest contributions to English landscape gardening. Although the folly is called the Convent, and indeed has twelve niches in the drawing room which originally contained painted panels of nuns, it was never lived in by a religious order, nor had it any other ecclesiastical purpose. Rather, as one of the owners, architect Christopher Bowerbank, said, 'there is about it a hint of profanity'.

The Convent is romantically sited near the top of a hill surrounded by soft woodland, and for all its eccentricity is actually a Grade I listed building – the highest preservation order allotted in the United Kingdom. Unfortunately this designation did little to help its preservation. When Mr Bowerbank and his co-owner and business partner, Peter Lacey, first saw it, it had been appallingly vandalized. The drawing-room floorboards had been ripped up and burned, and the resulting charcoal used to scrawl scatalogical graffiti on the walls. The stained glass had been stolen from the Gothic windows, the fireplace had been removed, and the singular vaulted ceiling made from small stones pressed into horsehair plaster in the manner of a grotto had been painted white, which, although not strictly vandalism, was an insensitive thing to do when the original stones 'had glistened like gold when touched by the sun', according to a local builder long familiar with the house.

For 200 years the place had been lived in by a motley variety of gamekeepers and labourers until earlier in this century when it was leased from the Hoares by an eccentric called Gervase Smith. He led the life of a hermit in the Convent, lost in an alcoholic haze judging by the detritus of bottles found in the garden. When he died, the succeeding tenant moved two large vanloads of rubbish from the undergrowth and started a wholly unimpressive two-storey extension made of ugly concrete blocks and steel windows before giving up halfway through the exercise. For the next ten years the house stood forlorn and empty. Then the National Trust offered a generous lease to anyone who would undertake sensitive restoration.

For all its lamentable state, the new owners, now joined in their venture by Sarah and Jamie Maclean,

Opposite: *The Convent glimpsed through the garden*. Top left: *Gothic bay window*.
Left: *The dining room*.

37

were entirely beguiled by the house, its position, its views, its interior spaces – which turned out to be much larger than would appear from the exterior – but most of all by its roof. On the west front there are two towers surmounted by curious skeletal pyramids with *fleur-de-lys* finials. And the central chimney is disguised by an enormous obelisk standing on a plinth, surrounded by four smaller ones corbelled out from the central structure. Finally, there is a bell tower which was such a blissful haunt for bees that forty pounds (18 kg) of honey was extracted during the renovation.

The first consideration was to get some water to the property since there were no main services, nor was there even a well in the vicinity. However, the Hoare estate gave permission for the use of the water from two springs about a quarter of a mile (0.5 km) away from the house but way down the hill. The enterprising owners found a man in Cornwall who made waterwheels, dammed up the springs, built a catchment tank and connected the waterwheel to a pump. This pumps water slowly back up the hill to an enormous tank.

An extraordinary Wamsler cooker, said to be 'by appointment to King Ludwig of Bavaria', heats all the hot water and radiators as well as providing cooking power. However, installing electricity proved impossibly expensive, so it was decided to stick to candles and oil lamps which, in any event, provide an appropriately romantic light for the rooms.

The whole renovation took a year to complete. The concrete blocks were stuccoed and thus happily disguised. All the inappropriate steel windows were taken out of the new extension and replaced with graceful substitutes with Gothic heads. Fortunately, there was just enough original windows left in the main structure to copy the pattern exactly and Charlie Janson, Sarah Maclean's brother, was able to make exquisite new versions. The small diamond-shaped panes are hand-made cast glass in alternating colours of pale green and purple. And since an eighteenth-century account of the building refers to a fly to be found within the panes, they replaced the fly and added a spider.

Many other elements were taken from the eighteenth-century building and reinterpreted in the restoration, such as the staircase balustrading with its stylized Gothic arches, and the drawing-room fireplace with obelisks at either end. In its revived state the interior would surely give much pleasure to its visionary creator, Mr Hoare.

Left: *The drawing room, with its vaulted ceiling and Gothic windows.*

French Country House

Tucked away in the countryside near Paris is one of those dreamlike French houses set in an ancient park at the end of a tree-lined *allée*, or drive, where the branches meet and twine overhead like the vaulted ceiling of a cathedral. Although it looks as if it could have been standing there for centuries, it only dates back less than a hundred years. It is, in fact, an exquisite late nineteenth-century copy of a Louis XVI folly, or pavilion, built and furnished by a romantic antiquarian enthusiast on the ruins of a priory which was razed to the ground during the French Revolution.

There was an immense enthusiasm among certain people in France at the turn of the last century for all things eighteenth century. Just as many English Edwardians loved to copy Queen Anne buildings and furniture, so, too, the France of *La Belle Epoque*, with all its indulgence in luxury and its insouciant, slightly decadent atmosphere, indulged in pre-Revolutionary aesthetic tastes.

The charm of this house owes much to its surroundings. Park and house are in a way inseparable, magical at any season. In the autumn the house looms through a veil of mist rising from the Seine. The air is spicy with woodsmoke, the trees are beaded with dew, and the esoteric collection of seventeenth-century statues and urns gleam through the tangle of tawny leaves at the end of an arbour, or in a clearing in the woods. In the winter, when the place is blanketed in snow, the strong, solid lines of the columns on the facade are framed by the skeletal shapes of trunks and branches all around; and the house appears etched sharply against the prevailing white, while the park resounds with the cries of toboggan and cross-country ski parties. In spring and summer the house is sensuously enveloped in an intensity of greens, its occupants lazing on the flowered terrrace, or sitting on one of the white marble benches in the cool of the shade under a tree.

But the house is magical not only because of its ravishing setting, the architectural equivalent of Sleeping Beauty, or *La Belle au Bois Dormant* as the French say more melodically, but because the owners have perfectly preserved the serenity and grandeur of its rooms while filling them with life, warmth and a palpable domesticity. However much of the house is devoted to the past or, one might say, an *idea* of the past, it is also quite clearly lived in and enjoyed.

For almost a century nothing has changed except for the occasional replacement of a curtain or upholstery

Left: *The house seen from its park. The romantic surroundings contrast with the crisp lines of the drive and the columned facade.* Above: *Geraniums, massed in a sunny spot, winter indoors.*

fabric when it was absolutely necessary, and the careful interjection of good lighting to bolster the original candelabra and sconces, and in particular to display the paintings. The house shows quite definite signs of wear and tear, albeit elegantly faded wear and tear. But then it is also a spendid record of the way life was, the fabrics that were produced, the window treatments, types of upholstery and furniture arrangements that were fashionable in the late nineteenth century. It is not so much a domestic museum – for that implies a freezing or suspension in time – as a living documentary. Although there is a rigid adherence to the aesthetics of a time past with no real concession to the present, the formality of the house is treated as a unique background to be used with spirit rather than with too restrained a respect.

The dining room may have a magnificent early Chinese carpet, elaborate console tables and mirrors, imposing busts and a painting by the school of Poussin

Top: *In the Winter Garden*, Belle Epoque *armchairs provide comfortable seating among plant-filled* jardinières. Above: *Screens and flowers soften the formality of the furniture.*

along with a nineteenth-century English portrait, but the long and graceful windows open onto views of Arcadian bliss and the walls ring with the talk and animation of family and frequent guests.

Elegantly arched glass doors connect the 'Winter Garden' to the Grand Salon. The Winter Garden is a little salon filled with plants and Napoleon III *Belle Epoque* armchairs, with a marble floor and a casually comfortable air. The entrance to the Grand Salon is flanked by two marble columns which frame an old fountain sunk into the marble floor and an eclectic array of splendid furniture, from a Louis XIV console table to more Napoleon III armchairs of the same period as the house. Countering the formality of this room and the grandeur of its furniture, beautiful old *jardinières* full of plants and vases full of flowers overflow with life, and the fountain, which is in perfect working order, adds movement and sparkle.

Top: *The grandly-furnished dining room, with its chandelier and elaborate mirrors.* Above: *A marble bust stands before a mirror reflecting the handsomely draped arched window.*

All over the house groupings of furniture and paintings are softened by flowers, or a skilfully placed screen, or by gentle colours. A bedroom might contain rather grand Louis XVI beds but these are tempered by a cane table and chair, a floor lamp with a floppy silk shade. Deep window embrasures are lightened by soft Austrian blinds; arched windows are set off by softly tied-back curtains and draperies. The bathrooms have handsome early basins and baths and are carefully accessorized to bring them gently into the twentieth century. Splendid busts and paintings are to be found everywhere.

Someone described the house and its park as midway between the Barbizon school with its Arcadian landscapes and the *douceur Proustienne* of turn-of-the-century salon life. The house has indeed a Proustian echo, a real remembrance of times past. But it is also very much a house that is lived in and enjoyed in the present.

Left: *The Grand Salon*. Right: *Upstairs hallway*.
Below: *Cane furniture and antique beds*.

*O*ne of the acknowledged ways of successfully being able to safeguard part of one's historical heritage and maintain a great house in the late twentieth century is to run it both as a home and as company headquarters. Château de Bachen in Les Landes, now the registered offices of Michel Guérard Conseil SA as well as the home of Michel and Christine Guérard, their two small daughters and their office staff, vineyard workers and housekeepers, is a shining example of just such a practical merger.

More particularly, it is a dream come true for Madame Guérard. In 1967, as a young girl, Christine Barthelemy first set eyes on the house, tried and failed to buy it. Sixteen years later she finally achieved her ambition when she was able to buy the house with her husband.

Michel Guérard is the famous co-founder of *La Nouvelle Cuisine* and the creator of *La Grande Cuisine Minceur*, which he developed after studying his father-in-law's clients dieting at Eugénie les Bains, the spa christened by Empress Eugénie, the beautiful and influential wife of Napoleon III. *La Cuisine Minceur*, or 'slimming cuisine', is the first food devised for dieters which is as delicious as it is low on calories. Because it is so sophisticated, no gourmets who need to watch their weight should ever feel deprived. Clients who now flock to the Guérards' renowned hotel-restaurant and spa, Les

Left: *The Guérard kitchen-laboratory where Monsieur Guérard devises new recipes. The enormous cooker (stove) was made to the Guérards' specifications.* Above: *Château de Bachen.*

Prés et les Sources d'Eugénie, can enjoy the cuisine while they diet, and relax by taking the waters of the ancient thermal baths, in their splendid eighteenth-century setting.

Before Madame Guérard's marriage, her father, Adrian Barthelemy, had already entrusted the entire management of his spa and restaurant to her. As passionate about antique furniture and art as she is about food, Christine Guérard has had some twenty years of experience in the restoration and renovation of old houses, and these skills are spectacularly evident at Les Prés et les Sources d'Eugénie. This also meant that she knew the district well, so when she and her husband decided to try to find a beautiful house somewhere near their restaurant, it was with delight that they redis-

covered and were able to acquire the pastoral château with which Madame Guérard had been captivated sixteen years earlier.

Situated on a hill overlooking the Adour valley and reached by a magical *allée* shaded by rows of ancient oaks, the house stands on property which had been in the hands of the Barons de Pausader de Peich, Lords of Bachen, since the thirteenth century. Their ancestor was a courtier of Gaston Phoebus, Earl of Foix and Prince of Béarn, who was granted the right to fish along that stretch of the Adour river.

The château, built in the seventeenth century, had remained in the family for the last 350 years through its female descendants. During the early stage of its restoration, when old, encrusted cement was being removed

Above: *The panelled dining room with a view through to the library.* Right: *The library, with deeply embrasured windows and tapestry-covered walls, has a comfortable atmosphere. Madame Guérard searched all over France for the correct seventeenth-century details.*

from one of the chimneys, a small brick with a wolf sculpted on it came to light. This was the emblem of the first *seigneur des lieux*, or lord of the manor, Loup Aner de Bachen, in the year 1235. This discovery, which confirmed what was known of the house's history, delighted the Guérards, who decided not to replace the rendering so that the small sculpted brick might remain visible. And it also prompted them, if they needed prompting, to name the house Château de Bachen.

Christine Guérard, at last in possession of her dream house, took charge of its restoration and decoration. Previously long neglected, today the house enchants with its pure lines and perfect proportions which nevertheless give a curiously light-hearted effect. The Guérards were careful to replace the old-style exterior coating of limestone, fawn-coloured sand and charcoal wash which contrasts beautifully with the pristine white wooden shutters.

Inside, the house has been sensitively refurnished with seventeenth-century furniture and art, in keeping with the period of its origin. The artisans who helped with the restoration travelled all over France in search of authentic materials with which to duplicate the original atmosphere. The rooms are full of lovely details, old inlaid parquet floors and panelling, handsome fireplaces, and long graceful windows set into deep embrasures. To these, Christine Guérard has added her unique collection of eighteenth- and nineteenth-century full-length portraits, still-life and animal pictures, picked up over the years and now reposing throughout the house.

Not surprisingly, since the château now houses all Michel Guérard's food-related activities as well as his private living space, one of the most important rooms in the house is the kitchen. This is really a laboratory where Monsieur Guérard constantly invents and tests new recipes, experimenting with the new multi-purpose cooker (stove) that he and Madame Guérard designed and which they asked Molteni, the manufacturer of the Grand Chef, to produce. A smaller version of this stove will soon be available to the general public. The room with its flagged stone floor, *régence* panelling cupboard, handsome Louis XIV dining/work table, copper pans, sturdy wood shelves and hanging lamps is a delight to the eye as well as being a pleasure to work in.

The formal dining room with its wood-panelled walls,

Top right: *The staircase with whitewashed walls and waxed wood*. Right: *An elegant bedroom, with a brass four-poster bed, hung with white to match the soft furnishings*.

round table and inset vitrines is a charming place, as good to look at as it must be to eat in. The floor, like that in the library and salon, is composed of warm mellow terracotta tiles, with an inset diamond pattern.

The library, which immediately adjoins the dining room, has the same quiet composure. Colours are muted and subtly coordinated, with the panelled chimney breast painted white, providing a fresh contrast. A blazing fire, fabric-covered walls – matching the cloth on the dining table – and fine old rugs generate an atmosphere of warmth and intimacy. The treatment of the staircase which soars up gracefully through the house is typical of the way the entire house has been decorated: whitewashed walls, and quicklime-coated and waxed wood – simple and appropriate materials.

Upstairs rooms, too, are spectacularly, elegantly simple. The bedroom pictured here, for example, has a brass four-poster bed hung with white cheesecloth, matching the crisp white bedspread and the white *chaise-longue*, effectively contrasting with the beautiful inlaid parquet of the floor, the handsome inlaid desk and early portraits of noble ladies. Similarly, the bathrooms, with their white marble floors and extraordinary bathroom fixtures, are an object lesson in sensitivity, totally in keeping with the atmosphere of the house.

Despite the house's many functions, the business activities combine unobtrusively with the living quarters. Of course, the château is quite big enough to absorb official reception rooms, laboratories, offices, guest rooms and a separate guest apartment as well as a library, sitting rooms and the family bedrooms, but all have been harmoniously integrated.

In the same way, the grounds of the château subtly marry business with pleasure. While the Guérards' two young daughters find it all a perfect playground, the estate also works for its living. Beyond the garden and oak trees, the Guérards have carefully introduced a new vineyard. By mixing different vines, and with the aid of various vinicultural experts, they are trying to develop the taste of the eventual wine long before harvesting takes place. The *cru*, a white wine of that splendid Tursan variety which was renowned at the court of Eleanor of Aquitaine, will have its first harvest in 1989, and will be called 'Baron de Bachen', after its beautiful home ground.

Top left: *A splendid marble bath with a spectacular pair of mirrors.* Left: *Another bathroom view, with well-judged juxtaposition of surfaces.*

Reddish

eddish, the late Sir Cecil Beaton's house in
Wiltshire, is one of those perfectly symmetrical,
exquisite English eighteenth-century houses that
so many people dream of owning. Built of faded rose
brick and honey-coloured stone, it sits among tranquil
gardens on the sunny side of a hill, just outside a
charming village that is forever England. Reddish was
reputedly built by King Charles II for dalliance – as a
love nest – and it was Cecil Beaton's beloved home for
half a century or more.

'I enjoy feathering my nests,' Beaton is said to have
remarked when asked about his decorating prowess.
Great photographer and stage designer that he was, he
liked to transform wherever he lived into ultimate sets
for living, paying, of course, due attention to the
predominant style of the original framework but always
making the rooms essentially Beaton in feeling.

He also loved gardens. Francis Bacon called the love
of gardens 'the purest of human pleasures', a sentiment
shared by Beaton. The garden at Reddish with its
arbours, clipped box hedges, fine old trees, smooth
lawns, sweet-smelling flowers, mossy banks and lambent
stretches of water, with a congenial grouping of thatched

cottages and barns in the background, is pure delight.
From the spring onwards garden scents waft through
open windows and every room looks over a different
gentle vista.

'How clever of you, Sir Cecil,' the Queen Mother is
said to have confided to him on a visit, 'to have made
everything *look* so shabby.' It is this comfortable, lived-
in ambience which makes the house so particularly
English. Superficial signs of wear are tolerated and even
encouraged as proof of continuity, but underneath it all
is careful stage-management.

The whole house, in fact, with its contrasts of style
and mood, is like a series of atmospheric backdrops. Not
surprisingly, since Sir Cecil, stage-struck from an early
age, designed many theatrical sets. Even his photographs were often highly orchestrated, and it is clear that
a delight in the positioning of objects, art and furniture
has permeated his work.

He was particularly interested in the Edwardian era.
Almost an Edwardian himself (born in 1904) he was
obviously attracted to turn-of-the-century frivolity,
saying of that period that it was his 'stock in trade'.

A logical extension of Beaton's interest in photo-

Above: *Reddish, seen appropriately through a bower of roses. It was built by Charles II as a love
nest.* Right: *In the entrance hall, the floor, composed of worn flagstones, creates a rustic
contrast to the architectural formality of the moulded ceilings and marble columns, and Sir Cecil
Beaton heightened this with 'random' groups of plants, flowers and hats.*

graphy and stage design were his assays into interior decoration. He much admired Elsie de Wolfe, Syrie Maugham and Sybil Colefax, three influential decorators in the early decades of the twentieth century who managed to reconcile the rising spirit of Modernism with the period-piece interiors which owners of country houses had inherited from their Victorian predecessors. This combination of forward-thinking experiment and nostalgia also characterizes Beaton's work.

The entrance hall to the house is cool and spacious. The floor is laid with worn flagstones and the walls are fine stucco with elegant mouldings and greenish marble pillars. In Sir Cecil's time it was always full of baskets of flowers, pots of flowering plants, trugs full of cut flowers, walking sticks and an endless supply of hats. Sir Cecil always wore hats: they were his trademark.

Cecil Beaton shared Reddish with his mother, who lived there with him until she died. For her he added on the much-photographed, beautifully planted conservatory, with its damp foliage, wet earth smell. It is a folly with Gothic arched windows, leaf-green walls, and a soaring glass roof veined with bamboo.

In complete contrast, the library, nicely filled with

books, is warm and comforting with touches of red velvet. There are chintz couches and chairs and a plethora of potted plants and flowers.

The drawing room is an Edwardian fantasy of glazed chintz and fine French furniture, *bergères*, sconces and gilded mirrors. A benign turn-of-the-century portrait of Mrs Beaton in an elaborate frame smiles gently over all.

Another abrupt change of mood is provided by the dining room, a rather spare space with whitewashed walls, and bronze sculptures by Giacometti, as well as several skeletal lamps. Sir Cecil's own bedroom has a vast four-poster bed, 'made up of this and that', centred in the middle of the room which is otherwise filled with *toile de Jouy*, antiques, and memorabilia of all kinds.

The whole house, in fact, is filled with such memorabilia, portraits of Sir Cecil by Augustus John, Christian Bérard (whom Beaton admired extravagantly), and David Hockney, all at different stages of his life. These are set amongst drawings and paintings from the eighteenth, nineteenth and twentieth centuries which Beaton collected over the years. 'But that is what it is all about', as Sir Cecil used to say. 'Decorating should be, must be, the reflection of a person and his preferences.'

Top: *The 'Edwardian' drawing room.*
Opposite: *Sir Cecil Beaton's pastoral conservatory-folly, built for his mother who shared his home. It has arched windows, Gothic in design, pale green walls and a glass roof, and a small pond set into the floor. The room overflows with plants.*

Massachusetts Farmhouse

Robert Liberman always wanted a house set deep in the countryside, by water. He had lived in, walked around, and ridden over the densely-wooded hilly country on the Massachusetts-Connecticut border for some years when circumstances forced him to give up his old Greek revival farmhouse in the area. Then, riding through the woods one day, he came across a forty-acre (16 hectares) swamp with old trees sticking eerily up from the shallow water. Centuries before in the Glacial Age, he discovered, this swamp had been a deep lake; since it was beautifully sited in the cleft of three hills the idea came to him to restore the lake and build a house right next to it.

He and his wife knew exactly what they wanted. Their home had to have the feeling of an old farmhouse with small connecting rooms, look unpretentious and rural, yet have none of the traditional inconveniences of such old properties: that is to say, the Libermans wanted the heating to work properly, bathrooms off each of five bedrooms and the house to be thoroughly practical and easy to run.

*Above and right: The Libermans' dream house,
deep in the New England
countryside. The wooden structure blends happily
into the mass of the woods behind.
Old stone walls were discovered on the site.*

Not a man to haver around, Robert Liberman bought the swamp and as much surrounding acreage as he could. He then started a five-and-a-half-year marathon of clearing woodland, dredging, landscaping and building. The first task was to clear the land and build a road for access. Apart from the lake site, he cleared some seventy or eighty acres (about 30 hectares), a mammoth undertaking in itself.

What no one had been prepared for, however, was the disposal of some 600,000 yards (540,000m) of peat that needed to be dredged up from the swamp. It was a nightmare. Eventually they rolled a good deal of the wet peat down a hill and grew pasture on top; they dried as much as they could of the rest and sold it. But for several years great mounds of the stuff stood around like primeval relics. But there were rewards as well. About fifteen feet (4.5m) below the surface of the swamp they came across an old beaver dam which, judging from its

depth below the surface, must have been at least a thousand years old. The excavation also threw up old animal bones, ancient tools, farm implements and the detritus of centuries, before the Libermans finally achieved what they wanted – a spectacular stretch of water some thirty-five feet (10.5m) deep.

The next step was the landscaping and the siting of the house. Frank Lloyd Wright noted in his autobiography that 'no house should ever be *on* any hill or on anything. It should be *of* the hill, belonging to it, so hill and house could live together, each the happier for the other'. Robert Liberman clearly had the same point of view. For him everything had to be intuitive, organic. He knew he should *feel* how the land and house should look and be connected. And to this end he spent hours just wandering, or consulting with his sensitive landscape architect, Wallace Gray, not afraid to change his mind from one week to another if he had a better

Above: The library with green-coloured walls, decorated with antlers and horns.

thought, or if the work he commissioned did not turn out quite as he had anticipated.

One bitter winter weekend, when he and architect Mark Hampton were trudging around with camera and yellow pad discussing the position of the house and almost up to their hips in snow, they suddenly knew exactly where the house would be sited. They returned home and in about three and a half hours Mark, with, as Bob Liberman said, his great eye for details, vistas and a comfortable whole, produced a sketch of how the house should look, followed by a dimensional drawing. And it was to that basic design and drawing that the house was built, almost entirely by the Libermans' caretaker. The services were left to professionals to instal, but otherwise the house was put together by one man, with Bob and Barbara Liberman making all the crucial decisions as the building progressed.

As it happened, the Libermans discovered that

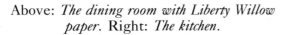

Above: *The dining room with Liberty Willow paper*. Right: *The kitchen*.

another farmhouse had stood on much the same site years before, which accounts for the original old stone walls they found nearby. But the new house looks so much as if it has always been part of the landscape that people congratulate them on their sensitive renovation.

The house is built almost entirely of dark seasoned wood, with one stone wing for the Libermans' bedroom. 'It looks rather like an old lodge,' Bob Liberman says, 'with a stone keeping room off one end, and in a way seems rather French with the sharp pitch of the gables and dormers'. In winter, the house melds almost imperceptibly into the woods behind, and the lake, which normally laps near the stone walls of the swimming pool right in front of the house, is covered with a deep layer of snow.

Inside, they have all the small rooms they wanted, eat-in kitchen, dining room, sitting room, library-den, hall, bedrooms and bathrooms, each with a comforting fireplace, and each, downstairs at least, opening off one another. Some rooms are left with natural wood walls, some are painted, some papered. Wood floors, too, are left plain with area rugs for comfort and downstairs

windows are left uncovered. All rooms are full of the Libermans' idiosyncratic collections of this and that: old mirrors hanging on the library walls; old tools, instruments and horseshoes excavated from the swamp; paintings; toys, prints, antlers, horns, boxes, old country furniture, wooden articulated models, old wooden objects and carvings. As Robert Liberman says, there is much more focus on the things themselves, than how they fit into a scheme. Both he and his wife are inveterate picker-uppers of the curious, the strange (note some of the unusual chairs) and almost any sort of wooden bygone. They collect pieces in France as much as America, England as much as Italy, in small country towns as much as in Manhattan.

The house does seem rooted: full of children and dogs, with wonderful views from the windows and terrace across the lake and through the woods. Rooms smell aromatically of woodsmoke and flowers and leaves. 'It is my dream,' says Robert Liberman. 'Some people call it my folly, and I can see what they mean. I can see their point of view. But it is now exactly what I wanted, from the shoreline around the lake to the house itself.'

Left: A view of the main living room. Walls have a natural finish. Note the antler candelabra, the old toys. Top left and top right: Two more views of the living room with a collection of old tools, horseshoes and curios found on the land. The large window overlooks the lake.

THE PAST RELIVED

We two kept house, the Past and I
The Past and I
I tended it while it hovered nigh

THOMAS HARDY

Villa Kerylos

To have an obsession is one thing. To have enough money to carry out your obsession is quite another. Théodore Reinarch, a brilliant and eccentric Frenchman at the turn of the century, was both an ardent Hellenist and extremely rich. He made use of these two attributes by building a perfect replica of an ancient Greek villa on an airy promontory in Beaulieu, just east of Cap Ferrat.

Reinarch's absorption in Greek civilization was so great that he insisted on living in the house in exactly the same way as the early sophisticated Greeks would have lived. He even made his guests wear the clothes and adopt the habits of ancient Greece.

'Hellenism', he wrote in 1902, 'is to the world of ideas what radium is to that of nature: at any age it will revive and rejuvenate us. . . . Even after 3,000 years their work has a contagious youthfulness.'

To build the house, Reinarch chose as his architect Emmanuel Pontremoli, a member of the Academy of Fine Arts, a recipient of the Grand Prix de Rome, and his intellectual equal in Hellenistic enthusiasm. Pontremoli had been devoting himself to the study of Asia Minor, particularly Pergamum, with a view to the restoration of the acropolis at Didyma and to the complete reconstruction of the Temple of Apollo.

Instead, from 1902 to 1908, he was lured into designing Reinarch's house with the brief that it was to be in a pure style, similar in feeling to the houses merchants or ship-owners of Delos or the Cyclades might have owned, overlooking the sea where they could watch for the return of their vessels. It was to be called 'Kerylos', a Greek word meaning 'tern', and was to be constructed in natural materials: stone, marble, bronze, ivory and wood. Although the ancient Greeks covered their windows with parchment and oiled papyrus, Reinarch decided to compromise with blown glass; he also conceded to the comforts of modern plumbing, running water and electricity provided that they were well concealed.

Pontremoli succeeded brilliantly in capturing Reinarch's vision of the past. Visitors feel they are actually in an ancient Greek villa that has somehow been immaculately preserved through the centuries. The marble, alabaster and bronze statues, the extraordinarily elaborate mosaic floors, the frescoes of mythological

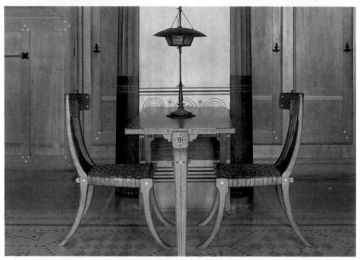

Top right: *The marble cloister looking over the atrium.* Centre: *Table and chairs in the library.* Right: *Reinarch's red bedroom, with Pompeian bed.* Opposite: *The grand salon.*

events, the perfect reproduction of the form of such a house, all contribute to this uncanny sensation.

As in the fifth century BC, the main living rooms are all arranged around an atrium, or internal courtyard, open to the blue sky of the Côte d'Azur. Twelve Doric pillars in brilliant white Carrara marble forming a peristyle, or cloister, surround this courtyard, where a rose-laurel, Apollo's tree, is watered by a tinkling fountain.

On one side of the atrium is Reinarch's library, with all its windows looking east over the Mediterranean to accommodate Reinarch's preference for working in the morning. One and a half storeys high, it is filled with artefacts found at excavations, and furniture designed by Pontremoli of oak inlaid with ivory, or of boxwood or ebony. Leather reclining swan chairs are modelled on an Egyptian chair in the Louvre, and the high desks are designed to be stood at, for in ancient Greece that is how people used to work.

Ancient vases, statuettes and oil lamps stand on tables and chests; Pontremoli also designed a special bronze chandelier for the room, as indeed he did for every room. Names of Greek writers are inscribed on the wall, and around the top of the room a broad frieze is stencilled and painted in an elaborate Greek key pattern. Best of all is Reinarch's own inscription: 'Here, with Greek orators, sages and poets, I have built a peaceful retreat in immortal beauty!'

Off the atrium, too, are the dining room, or *triklinos*, and the grand salon, men's sitting room, or *andron*. The latter is furnished in a similar style to the library, with the addition of a 'throne' for the master of the house, inspired by paintings on Greek vases. The walls are faced with Tuscan marble and the wooden ceiling is splendidly decorated. Even the utensils in the dining room are made of the same clays and oxides used in Greek pottery. Pontremoli rejected modern crystal for the glasses and had goblets made in irregularly coloured Venetian glass. The Reinarchs and their guests ate reclining on couches with a deep frieze of styled trees around them topped by a magnificent blue and gold beamed ceiling.

Reinarch and his wife had their private suite of rooms up on the next floor, reached by a white marble staircase. It consists of two bedrooms, their adjoining bathrooms, and a central rest room, or small sitting room, called the

Left: *A view of the library, with the swan chairs based on an Egyptian design in the Louvre.* Top right: *The dining room. Guests ate on couches.* Right: *The small sitting room.*

triptolème. This last is painted to resemble a Greek garden with an especially elaborate mosaic floor modelled on one in the Dolphin House at Delos.

The ceiling of Mrs Reinarch's columned bedroom is painted a light blue with a hanging made by Ecochard, while the recesses behind the columns are a deep blue decorated with peacocks, the emblem of Hera, the goddess of marriage. Théodore Reinarch's room is in Pompeian red, and the bronze and wood bed is a copy of one actually found at Pompeii.

Each bathroom has a marble bath in the form of a plumbed-in sarcophagus with concealed taps, all designed by Pontremoli. Bronze handbasins stand on tripods and are without running water. A shower, bidets, lavatories, even mirrors are all concealed behind door panels and closets.

There were also more elaborate bathing arrangements for the household. Just off the main entrance to the villa is a columned bath-house or *balaneion*, housing an enormous sunken plunge bath with taps concealed under bronze covers. In the centre of an archway at the end of the room is a niched basin. Walls, floor, basin and bath are all formed from polished Carrara marble.

Théodore Reinarch lived in his sunlit ancient Greek villa working on various esoteric theses and a new demonstration of Pythagoras' Theorem until his death in 1928 when he was sixty-eight – a good age for an ancient Greek. He bequeathed Kerylos, his perfect reproduction, to the Institut de France for the benefit of future Hellenists, although it was not actually listed by the Department of Historic Monuments until 1967. Now, however, it is open to the public throughout the year and anyone may go to Beaulieu-sur-Mer and marvel at the glory that was Greece.

Top left: The splendid bath-house off the main entrance, with a sunken marble plunge bath. Taps are concealed under bronze covers. Top right: A shower, one of the modern facilities that did not exist in ancient Greece but designed to classical proportions and in the magnificent materials found throughout the villa. Opposite: Mrs Reinarch's columned bedroom.

$\mathcal{G}$eorgian $\mathcal{R}$estoration

The Hudsons had always wanted a Georgian house in Worcestershire, England and, being both patient and philosophical, were prepared to wait till they found exactly that without compromise. Happily, they saw the potential in a house that no one else seemed to see.

Superficially, it is true, the house seemed too large, too dark, too full of gloomy corridors and smallish rooms, with hideous modern windows and a tacked-on Victorian porch. But, on the other hand, it had a beautiful garden tucked into an unspoilt valley with rolling hills on every side. They knew that they could make the house as fine as its surroundings, even if the renovation took years to achieve. Because the position was so superb, the Hudsons held out very little hope of affording the house when it came up for auction and they were therefore as much surprised as delighted when they walked away owning the place.

But restoration did take years. To start with, the Hudsons knocked down several of the passage walls on the ground floor to let in more light. Because the entrance hall was long and thin, they removed the wall dividing it from the dining room to make a more generous space. They found a local craftsman to copy windows from the one original that was left, and then replaced all the unsympathetic ones. They removed the Victorian porch and replaced it with pillars and a portico.

They laid black and white marble tiles in the hall, and flagstones, where appropriate, over most of the ground floor. In the kitchen they laid Cotswold stone tiles (but upside down because they looked better that way). Now, unsealed but heavily polished, they only needed the occasional waxing and are able to withstand the wear of country life beautifully.

Two small rooms were knocked into one to make a library and two wooden pillars now flank its entrance. Originally intended for the porch, these arrived too small for that position, but turned out, by some miracle, to be precisely the right height for indoors. Bookshelves were inset into the walls and two alcoves were discovered when the Hudsons were tapping the plaster to see if anything interesting was hidden behind.

All this structural work took many months, during which time the Hudsons were living in a cottage

Left: *The dining room with Mrs Hudson's mural painting above mantelpiece, showing two imaginary figures against a landscape background, actually the views from the drawing room. She also painted the sky and clouds on the ceiling.* Above: *The house stands in beautiful gardens, set in unspoilt, rolling countryside.*

conveniently in the grounds. When, finally, the last load of dirt and rubble was removed, Jill Hudson, who trained as a painter, moved in to do a good deal of the decorating.

First she sponge-stippled the library and then tackled the walls of the adjoining small sitting room which she treated in the same manner. The next task was the kitchen. She could not find enough old doors for the sort of kitchen cabinets that she wanted so she bought new units, stripped them of all their polyurethane gloss – a task that took three weeks in itself – then sanded them down to roughen the wood a little and wiped white chalk into all the cracks to get the dusty old look she wanted.

After this triumph, she embarked on the lengthy task of marbling all the downstairs doors and the walls up to the dado rail. It took weeks of painstaking effort but when she had finished she knew it was not right. Courageously, she painted it all over in matt white and after that, she said, she concentrated on murals.

She took three weeks to execute a painting of sky and clouds on the dining-room ceiling, but once she was practised at balancing on a stepladder and painting above her head, she managed the next mural in the sitting room in half the time. The next job was to tackle the rather large space above the elaborate marble fireplace in the dining room. Almost before she knew it she was painting a large portrait in oils directly on the wall, of two imaginary figures standing in front of a green landscape which is actually the view from the drawing room.

Mrs Hudson's final act of imagination was to decorate the surfaces in a bedroom belonging to her grown-up son. She discovered an American paper with a strong colonial flavour, which she much liked and therefore ordered. It took nine months to come from the United States but that did not deter her. When it was finally up on the walls she painstakingly repeated its design on the panels of closet doors, accentuated the somewhat naive old look by adding a bedspread in the same design.

Now that the house is completely finished, the Hudsons have every sort of reward for being able to wait for what they thought was exactly right, without being prepared to compromise. All the rooms are exactly as they had hoped and they have the deep pleasure of knowing that they revived an old house and injected it with new life and verve.

Top left: *A corner of the drawing room.* Below:
*Pillars flanking the library entrance
were meant for the porch.* Right: *A bedroom.
Closet panels were painted by Mrs Hudson.*

Samode Palace

The wild and beautiful state of Rajasthan in India, with its geographic contrasts of great green forests and cool lakes, dry white miles of desert and dusty straggling villages, exotic gardens and steep cliffs of wild bougainvillaea, is as rich in forts and palaces as it is in history and dispossessed maharajahs. And the whole state can boast few more magnificent palaces than those in the vicinity of its capital of Jaipur.

Jaipur, or the 'Pink City', is so called because many of the buildings lining the unusually wide streets are of a striking oleander pink, deepening to a rosy terracotta. Visitors to Jaipur naturally gravitate to two outstanding examples of Indian architecture. The first is the City Palace, with its mixture of Moghul and Rajput styles, its glorious inner courtyards, and its *Hawa Mahal*, or Palace of the Winds. This is a lace-like five-storey building, only one room deep, but with 593 niches or windows, which was built in 1799 by a thoughtful maharajah so that the royal ladies in *purdah* could watch the world go by, without the world watching them.

Second on any tourist's itinerary would be the extraordinary fortress-palace of Amber, which seems to grow out of the rocky hill rising about Maota Lake, a cooling place for all types of wildlife, from cranes and buffaloes to the more domesticated ducks. Amber was built in 1592 by Raja Man Singh I, a commander in the Moghul Emperor Akbar's army, who rated prudence more highly than the approval of his fellow, perpetually tussling, Rajput princes. His prudence paid off in monetary rewards, not to mention royal alliances in marriage, and as a result Man Singh I was able to build the extraordinary buildings that he did. Behind the fierce and formidable ramparts and terraces, designed to be accessible by elephant, is an extraordinarily ornamented and mirrored interior, gleaming seductively in the light that filters through shuttered, louvered windows.

Left: *Grand council chamber with extraordinary ornamented walls, ceiling, pillars, floor and stonework, lit by a splendid chandelier.* Above: *The entrance to Samode Palace. Its light, almost frivolous exterior is in direct contrast to the craggy mountains that rise behind its romantic rose-ochre coloured walls.*

Top: *Detail of a beautiful archway.* Above:
Decorated shutters and stonework.

Yet, although both the City Palace and Amber are undoubtedly splendid examples of princely architecture, they pale beside the little-known, much more domesticated but perfect jewelled palace of Samode, hidden away in deepest country some twenty-five miles (42 km) from Jaipur. It was built at much the same time as Amber, in the late sixteenth century, and probably by the redoubtable Man Singh, though its origins are open to question. To reach it, you have to find your way up through mountainous country and narrow country roads until you come to the ancient village of Samode. The palace rears majestically and somewhat unexpectedly before you in all its pinky-ochre glory, frilled and trimmed with white around the arches and window embrasures, one of the few unspoilt preserves of the former maharajahs.

Until comparatively recently, the palace has been kept strictly private, secret, a well-hidden treasure of the last successors to the earlier *jaghirdars*, or lords, the Rawal Singhs. Lately, however, it has moved from complete obscurity to the full glare of media attention. Because of its singular beauty – the elaborately painted rooms, exquisite gilding, and remarkable *Sheesh Mahal*, or Hall of Mirrors, the most beautiful in Rajasthan – it was chosen as the principal setting for the British television production of M.M. Kaye's *The Far Pavilions*.

We can only wonder for whom it was originally built, and to whom we owe the inspiration for this exquisite vision, with its graceful proportions and almost indescribably delicate and beautiful inlay work. The Taj Mahal, as we know, was built with the greatest love by a heart-broken Shah Jahan as a memorial to his wife, Mumtaz, who, after seventeen blissful years of marriage, died giving birth to their fourteenth child. Was there any such story here? The extraordinary thing is that no one seems to know. All we can do is admire and marvel at the workmanship, the patterns, designs and colours of the beautiful interiors. We can also be thankful that, as a felicitous result of the passing of the Raj, so many of these palaces have been transformed into hotels by their princely owners, and it is now possible to stay in national treasures like these and feast on the visual pleasures for as long as one likes.

Coming from the twentieth century and the pragmatic West, it is hard to come to terms with the minds and artistic inspiration that produced such a layering of pattern upon pattern, such borders, intricate stonework, juxtaposition of colours and materials, such fantastical inlaying of semi-precious stones into the whitest of marbles. Did some brilliantly gifted architect mastermind all this, specifying the layering of every pattern, the use of every material and colour? Or did it just happen with the natural – but disciplined – imagination of remarkable craftsmen working as a team?

What is evident at Samode, as it is at other architectural monuments in Rajasthan, is the blending of Moghul and Rajput styles. Together, these two warrior peoples combined to create an architecture which has come to typify India before the arrival of the British.

The Moghuls were a Muslim dynasty, descended from Ghenghis Khan, who were great conquerors. They came to rule an empire that eventually extended from the north to the south of India. The Moghuls were also great builders – perhaps to immortalize their conquests – and built to last, with a dedication to quality. Their work, which reached a peak in the seventeenth century, reflects the influence of Islamic design, with its non-representational, mathematical patterning. (By Islamic law, no decoration or art can represent a living thing, except in stylized form; only God can create.)

The Rajputs were also warriors, but of the Hindu religion, and resisted the Muslim invaders fiercely, particularly so in Rajasthan. They left their own architectural monuments and, like the Moghuls, they invested in materials that resisted the effect of the climate.

However these two styles were reconciled, the harmony of decorated surfaces in Samode Palace remains a delight. Rooms open onto rooms, cool archways lead into cloisters, or into further groups of rooms, all patterned and inlaid and coloured in different combinations of texture and tone. Graceful carpet runners are laid on

Above: *Highly decorated, cloistered balcony running around the top of an open courtyard. The soft lilac-pink ceiling contrasts with the creamy marble beneath.*

marble floors that are sometimes as intricately worked as the ceilings above. Even the inside curves of arches along graceful arcades are each patterned with different designs of inlaid marble. And walls in what were once main council or audience chambers have pierced designs to enable the ladies of the *Zenana*, or women's quarters, to see and hear the ceremonies.

To make the walls shine, powdered marble, crushed eggshell and even pearls were added to the last coat of paint, and elaborately painted walls with floral dados and cornices are happily mixed with walls inlaid with precious and semi-precious stones. Doors are carved with arabesques inlaid with ivory, and some rooms are encrusted with *pachikari-kakam*, convex pieces of col-

Left: *Painted floral dados contrast with mosaic walls and geometric patterns.*
Below: *Note the Moghul/Persian influence in the brilliant azure blue of the designs.*

oured mirror glass set in patterns into the plaster, or with *meenakari* work, a form of enamelling.

In the courtyards in the comparative cool of the evenings, perfumed coloured waters once splashed from the fountains, mingling with the heavy night scent of the ubiquitous Indian jasmine and other sweet-smelling flowers. Samode Palace was designed to appeal to the sense of smell as well as touch and vision, a haven for its princely landowners on their journeys between domains. Today, descendants of the last Maharajah of Samode live in the palace, personally welcoming guests to their unique 'hotel'. They are still honoured with the title 'Rawal Saheb', in memory of a warrior ancestor who fought on after his head was severed.

Right: *This elaborately pierced wall allowed the ladies of the* Zenana *to hear and see what was going on in the public audience chambers.* Below: *Enamelled and mirrored walls.*

Chicago Townhouse

Finding the right style for a new house in an eclectic but historic city neighbourhood is bound to take time and considerable thought. An avant-garde late twentieth-century design would never be at home in an area where clapboard Greek revival cottages sit side by side with elaborate wood-trimmed Renaissance revival buildings with rusticated stone piles, and a five-unit row of brick houses by Louis Sullivan, one of the revered fathers of modern design in America.

This question of 'fitting in' with existing buildings is invariably a vexed point for architects who, not unnaturally, want their designs to make a significant statement. However, any good-mannered architect with the slightest respect for the past, if offered the chance of designing for such a site, would hopefully temper his natural creative energy with sensitivity to the surroundings, and try to find a way to build an outstanding and innovative house, but in a restrained as well as a distinguished fashion.

Chicago architect, Lawrence Booth, had always been sensitive to this issue, and this was precisely the challenge offered him when a young couple approached him to ask for a design for a house with 'a classical sensibility', to fit into a long narrow site in one of the city's designated historic areas. Mr Booth's first thought was that, of course, any good architect has to have a classical foundation. His second was that whatever the surrounding houses were like he would still make every effort to produce a building that was contemporary and American, even if it did have to have neo-classical overtones.

After all, Chicago, 'the windy city', has a long tradition of architectural innovation. After the Great Chicago Fire of 1871, much of the city had to be rebuilt, although happily a good number of old buildings survived. As a consequence of this disaster, which coincided with advances in steel technology, the city became a workshop for leading architects who included William Le Baron Jenney, Dankmar Adler and Louis Sullivan. Precursors of the Modern Movement, these innovators worked mainly in the field of commercial architecture, using steel-frame construction to build higher than ever before. Sullivan's influence continued in the work of his famous pupil, Frank Lloyd Wright. These great architects, who had such an impact on the city, came to be known as the Chicago School.

Chicago's contribution to architecture has carried on throughout the twentieth century. Lake Shore Drive (1951) by Mies van der Rohe is a landmark of Chicago's

Left: *The impressive facade of the new house, with its generous glazing and interesting portico. The house was designed by architect Lawrence Booth and is located in an historic Chicago neighbourhood.* Above: *Limestone fireplace decorated in classic post-modernist colours in the family room.*

lakeshore. The Sears Tower (1974), taking up an entire city block, is still the tallest building in the world, while the First National Bank Plaza has the distinction of being the largest bank building. The 'magnificent mile' along Michigan Avenue, north of the Chicago River, is one of the most elegant shopping streets in America. And the remarkable collection of twenty-five houses designed by Frank Lloyd Wright for the suburb of Oak Park, where he had his own home and studio, attract many architectural pilgrims. The Chicago tradition, in short, is a hard act to follow.

The clients' request that Mr Booth try to get the maximum amount of daylight into the building was the pivot of his design, for a radical solution is needed to overcome the dark centre normally unavoidable in a long narrow site. His idea of coring out a large vertical skylit well from the centre of the proposed three-storey building was simple but inspired, and it enabled him to play around with all kinds of curved forms inside the framework of a traditional terraced (row) house shell.

Within the parameters that he had, Lawrence Booth managed to create an immensely elegant, formal-looking facade that has strong overtones of the past but is very much part of the present. Furthermore, it shares all the best qualities of its neighbours in terms of meticulous craftsmanship and a firm but restrained individuality. The house does stand out, but only because it is pleasing. Above all, it fits beautifully into the context of an historic neighbourhood, which is no mean feat.

The facade is executed in limestone and granite, and is as formal, symmetrical and elegant as any neoclassicist could wish. At the same time the large window above the impressive entrance, and the generous glazing, make the house seem warm and inviting as well, especially at night when the house is lit from within. Despite the formality and restraint, there is a great deal of vitality.

Through the entrance portico there is a glazed vestibule running the width of the house which gives an immediate impression of space and light. Internal windows separate this vestibule from the sitting room, and five steps lead up to the main level of the ground floor where the dining room and kitchen-family room behind it are sited.

Top left: *Looking from the library towards the master suite.* Left: *View from the first-floor landing to the vestibule below.* Right: *In the dining room the stair tread nosing is used flat on the walls.*

A pair of staircases rise from both of the long walls of the dining room; one from the front, one from the rear, and both are completely open to the central skylit well. The proportions and details of these stairs, with their small-gauge pipe railings and tread nosing carried round three sides and extended into half-round moulding applied horizontally to the walls, make them almost all the decoration needed in the room, and are a splendid riposte to eighteenth- and nineteenth-century detailing.

Four columns define the dining area, which is bounded on the short side by a low convex wall which looks over into the kitchen-family room with its enormous and beautifully detailed window. From this dining room the space soars up to the skylight above and the room is flooded with natural light during the day, and with subtle, fluid lighting at night.

The kitchen-family room is the least symmetrical room in the house. This is mainly because of a spiral stair opposite the interesting limestone fireplace – the staircase had to be installed to meet fire regulations.

There are many spectacular views created by these various intriguing facets of the interior. The best are undoubtedly either from the stairwell of the first and second floors looking down to the marble floor of the vestibule below, or looking back from the library on the first floor (whose large window is placed immediately above the portico) past the stairwell and the circular cut-out for night lighting, to the master suite beyond.

The various configurations of shapes, from the sharply defined mouldings around the library entrance, to stepped half-pillars either side of doors are impressive, as are the curved forms throughout the house – barrel vaults, concave screens walls and circular light cut-outs – which gently define or enclose the various interior spaces. These shapes, allied to the colours chosen from a palette of fifteen different shades of pinks, melons, blues, greeny-blues and creamy-whites, which change in intensity depending on the play of light, are wholly of the twentieth century, wholly contemporary. Despite this, the house still manages to convey the lightness of proportion of the early nineteenth century.

What Lawrence Booth and his project director, Keith Campbell, have achieved is the creation of a modern house that adds its own stature to an historic district. It, too, should be worth preserving in the future.

Opposite: *The dining room, showing the two staircases.* Top left: *Detail of a staircase.* Left: *A glazed panel separates vestibule from sitting room.*

Alnwick Castle

*T*he craggy border between Britain and Scotland has always been romantic, dramatic country patch-worked with sheep farms, wooded and wild in turns, with quick-running rivers and stormy coasts. Castles, keeps and towers are much in evidence, for this was marauding country and look-outs needed to be kept and lands defended.

The greatest of these border castles is Alnwick. Originally built in the twelfth to thirteenth centuries, Alnwick possesses the most complete 'barbican' or projecting watchtower of any English castle. It was later extended and renovated by Henry, the second Lord Percy of Alnwick, in the fourteenth century and much of his work is still in evidence.

In the second half of the eighteenth century, the Percys received the Dukedom of Northumberland and the first Duke commissioned James Paine and Robert Adam to transform his fortress into a palace. Adam had also been retained to remodel all the rooms on the main floor of a gentler southern house belonging to the Percys, Syon House in Middlesex, which he accomplished with conspicuous success, having just returned from Rome with a head full of the classical world.

Nevertheless, less than a century later, in 1855, Algernon, the fourth Duke, commissioned the Italian Montiroli, a well-known authority on *cinquecento* art and decoration, to produce interiors for Alnwick Castle modelled on the Roman palace style of the sixteenth-century Renaissance. Although the Percys left well enough alone at Syon House after Adam's transform-ation, Alnwick, one might say, is the product of a good many revivals of the past.

Montiroli undoubtedly made very grand rooms, full of spectacular furniture, much of which had already been acquired by the Percys. The ebony inlaid cabinet shown here, for example, is one of a pair said to have been purchased by the third Duke for one thousand pounds each. In the Northumberland House Book of 1875, there is a note saying that 'these cabinets belonged to Louis XIV and formed part of the furniture of one of the Royal Palaces under the old regime. They were accidentally discovered in a cellar in Paris, in which they were supposed to have been placed for safety during the Revolution'. Mounted with panels of different inlaid marbles and hard stones known as 'pietra dura', and decorated with mouldings of gilt copper and supported by chimerical legs resting on a carved and gilded wood

Right: *Alnwick Castle has undergone many changes since its construction in the twelfth century.*

stand, they were made by another Italian, Domenico Cucci, at the Gobelin factory for Louis XIV in 1683.

Montiroli's Music Room displays an astonishing wealth of decoration. The ceiling design was inspired by decorations in St Peter's Cathedral in Rome, and is of richly carved and gilded wood. The frieze, consisting of rich arabesques on a dark blue ground, was painted in Rome by Mantovani to a design by Montiroli, who also designed the carved doors.

Again, furniture and accessories are very elaborate. The chandelier, with its stem branches and festoons of glass, is from Northumberland House in London and is one of a pair, the other one of which hangs in the Red Drawing Room. Another pair shared between the two rooms are the nineteenth-century gilt Gobelin tapestry firescreens, purchased in Paris in 1849. The yellow shaped and serpentine-framed sofa with its three matching armchairs are part of a large set consisting of one sofa, fifty-four armchairs, twelve single chairs and six long stools. These are distributed all over the house and covered in various different materials such as silk damask, chintz and needlework.

Montiroli's Red Drawing Room is, if anything, even more splendid than the Music Room. The walls are covered with red damask ornamented with a gold pattern, and Montiroli used a collection of red and gilt furniture with tapered cylindrical legs in Louis XVI style, believed to have been designed by his predecessor, Robert Adam. The centrepiece is a white Carrara marble fireplace, supported by two caryatids.

The ceiling in this room consists of polygonal richly carved and gilded panels. Because of the intricate design, the original semi-circular bays formed by the castle's towers had to be converted to polygons during the restoration. It is unlikely that any contemporary designer would be able to effect such major structural alterations just for the sake of a ceiling design, but Montiroli clearly had a free hand and an exceedingly large budget.

All in all, this Renaissance revival is as dramatic in its way as its setting, the castle and surrounding countryside. Today, although some of the rooms are open to the public, the Percy family is still in residence. After six centuries of change and renewal, Alnwick has many pasts to offer.

Top left: *Detail of one of a pair of inlaid ebony cabinets made for Louis XIV.* Left:
The Music Room. Right: *The Red Drawing Room, remodelled by Montiroli.*

Oak Alley

Great Southern plantation houses, such as the immortal Tara in *Gone with the Wind*, have generally been considered the most romantic of homes. One thinks of cool and shady verandahs under massive porticos, fans languidly stirring the heavy air, a lingering scent of jacaranda, lofty ceilings, flagged floors and the deep green and white of Southern interiors.

Part of the image is that such places have been lovingly tended and handed on generation after generation. In fact, many of those erstwhile prosperous plantations came to untimely ruin – not just through the vicissitudes of the Civil War and the consequent reconstruction of the land, but through the sort of bad luck that one does not necessarily think of as contributing to economic misfortune. Swarms of insects and disastrous weather, along with the general economic depression of the South, all but finished off so many of the plantations in the late nineteenth century.

As a consequence, many of these great mansions had to be given up, to languish and crumble. Then, in the 1920s a handful of people with enough recognition of the historic and aesthetic value of the old plantations and, more importantly, enough money, embarked on programmes to save and restore them.

Oak Alley Plantation in Louisiana has had just such a chequered history. From the early 1700s, it has been the site of many people's dreams. At that time a French settler, lured by propaganda about Louisiana's many geographic and cultural advantages, chose a site on the Mississippi and, preparatory to building a grand house from which to enjoy his new rich life, very sensibly planted twenty-eight oak trees in two rows of fourteen, eighty feet (27m) apart, to form an avenue a quarter of a mile (0.5km) long leading to the river. He also set out the beginnings of a sugar plantation.

Alas, instead of the colonial opulence promised, the reality proved to be a primitive existence at best, with his grand house nothing but a hut at the end of a double

Left: Oak Alley seen from its inspiring avenue of oaks, now well over 250 years old. The house was beautifully renovated in the 1920s by Mr and Mrs Andrew Stewart, who restored and furnished the rooms with great sympathy for the original period. Above: The splendid verandah which helps to keep the house cool in summer.

arriving by steamboat down the river, and particular care was given to the garden. The final, magnificent result was proudly christened 'Bon Séjour', by Celina Roman, but travellers and steamboat captains floating by on the Mississippi, were so impressed by the avenue of oaks that they always called it 'Oak Alley' and so it remained.

The Roman family lived at Oak Alley for thirty years, all through the Civil War, but Jacques himself only lived seven years after the house's completion, dying in 1848. Unhappily his widow was endlessly extravagant, and the combination of the social and political turmoil resulting from the war and the draining expenditure meant that by the time Henri, the Romans' son, came of age and was able to assume responsibility for the property, it was really too late. For all his valiant efforts, in 1866 Henri was forced to sell the property at auction for a pittance.

A series of owners followed, but times were hard, with the sugar industry in deep decline. Eventually the house was boarded up and all its glory seemed doomed to collapse into the shadows of the oaks and the undergrowth. Then, in 1917, another bright-eyed aspiring owner came to Oak Alley, called Jefferson Davis Hardin Jr. He poured a fortune into the house and garden, and tried to turn the plantation into a model farm run by new scientific methods. For a few years the house bloomed. Then there was a series of disasters, including a costly court case arising from a train derailment when one of the Hardin cows wandered onto the line. Oak Alley had to be signed over to the Whitney Bank and once again it was shut up and left to rot.

Finally, and once again happily, it was bought in 1925 by Mr and Mrs Andrew Stewart who were among the first to start what has become a trend to save old properties such as this in that area of the South. The restoration took two years and cost $60,000, $10,000 more than the purchase price for the 1,360-acre (550 hectares) plantation. The Stewarts furnished the house sympathetically and treated each room with a kind of chaste sensibility, much in sympathy with the period the house was built. To ensure that Oak Alley would never fall into disrepair again, Mrs Stewart created a non-profit making trust. Upon her death in 1972 after forty-six happy years in the house, the mansion and twenty-five acres (10 hectares) of grounds passed to the foundation, who have kept it just as Mrs Stewart left it.

row of saplings. But the trees and the plantation flourished, even if its founder did not, and by 1836, when the newly married Jacques Telesphore Roman, brother of the Governor, and his wife Celina bought the estate, there was a magnificent alley of oaks, already more than a century old, leading to a perfect site for the mansion they intended to build.

The architect they chose was Celina's father, Gilbert Joseph Pilie, and the building took over two years to complete. The most notable feature of the house was the twenty-eight classic columns edging the verandah, built out thirteen feet (4m) from the walls to keep the house in the shade for most of the day. The bricks were made in pie-shaped moulds in order to achieve the circular form of the columns, and the walls throughout the house were sixteen inches (40cm) deep. Long windows and doors were carefully placed opposite each other for cross-ventilation, and marble was imported for floors.

Improvements and additions continued through the end of the decade; the kitchen was finally completed in 1841. All this time special furniture and fittings had been

Top left: *The dining room at Oak Alley decorated for the Christmas celebrations.* Top right: *A sitting room bears witness to the Stewarts' dedication to creating a period ambience for the house through the careful selection of objects and furniture.* Below right: *Two of the bedrooms which evoke a traditional American style. Furnishings include old handmade rugs and quilts.*

'Groombridge Place,' wrote the distinguished *Country Life* writer, Arthur Oswald, in 1955, 'is one of the loveliest houses in England.' From a man who wrote with erudition and a critical eye about country houses for the doyen of country house magazines, this was high praise.

Nor was he exaggerating. Groombridge is a lovely seventeenth-century moated manor house, situated in rolling, wooded country on the borders of Kent and Sussex, all mellow brick and weathered stone, with calm, still, reflecting water outside, and handsome panelling and furniture within. More rarely, in over 300 years there have been no additions, no embellishments, except for the gentle insertion of electricity, heating and plumbing. What you see now is what you saw then, but softened and refined by time into a near-lyrical composition of water, brick and garden. Although it has been lived in continuously since the Restoration, it has managed, miraculously, to preserve its quintessentially seventeenth-century character.

Left: *Groombridge Place – a graceful combination of old brick, trees and water.* Above: *Looking through the old windows to the garden.*

Groombridge Place, as it stands now, was built by Philip Packer, a lawyer, a founder member of the Royal Society, and a friend of Christopher Wren. It was erected some time between 1652 and 1676 on the site of a medieval house, the home of Philip Packer's father. We can date it within these twenty years or so, because Packer was also a friend of John Evelyn, the diarist, who was extremely fond of ordered nature and is said to have helped design the garden.

Evelyn recorded two visits to Groombridge, one to the old house, one to the new. In July 1652 he wrote: 'I heard a sermon at Mr Packer's chapell at Groombridge, a pretty melancholy seate, well wooded and water'd.... The chapel was built by Mr Packer's father, in remembrance of K. (ing) Charles the First, his safe returne out of Spain'. In August 1674, he describes the new Packer house as 'built within a moate in a woody valley'. 'The old house', he goes on to say, somewhat disparagingly, 'now demolished, and a new one built in its place, tho' a far better situation would have been on the South of the wood, on a graceful ascent.'

As a matter of fact, any other cultured man of the time would probably have made much the same observation. By the middle of the seventeenth century there was no need to build a house on a moated (or defensive) site in a valley bottom. For health and view alike, a situation on a hill was considered infinitely preferable. Further, what Evelyn saw would have been a new red brick house, with that slightly brash rawness that red brick has, surrounded by a moat, standing where an ancient medieval stone house had once been. The terraced garden to the north would still have been immature and in no way approaching the perfection that three centuries of careful tending, not to mention modern lawnmowers and hedge clippers have achieved. As Arthur Oswald put it, so succinctly:

'Time with its unimaginable touch has worked a miracle on a house, which, in the sort of setting that Evelyn had in mind, would have been just as homely and pleasing in its nice balance and proportions, but no more. Here,

Above left: *A view from the stairway.* Above right: *Wide porcelain washbasin coexists happily with seventeenth-century furniture. Henry Stanford Mountain, who bought Groombridge Place in 1919, was responsible for its 'modernization'.* Right: *The drawing room with its extravagant ceiling, fireplace and specially commissioned seventeenth-century panelling.*

Packers still hang. These portraits have always been sold with the house, although only two more generations lived on at Groombridge after Philip Packer died in 1686. The family finally settled in America

Two other local families lived there throughout the eighteenth and nineteenth centuries until 1919, when the house had the good fortune to be bought by Henry Stanford Mountain. Mr Mountain was a man of great taste and sensibility, with the money to indulge such tastes and sensibilities. He took a year modernizing the house, carefully installing amenities, like bathrooms, which had not existed before. He then spent the rest of his life, until his death in 1947, searching England for the right furniture, pictures, objects and hangings.

Mr Mountain's collection includes some outstanding successes. One particular piece is an inlaid cabinet of much the same date as the house, the doors of which have exquisite needlework panels on the inside, showing King Charles II and Queen Catherine of Braganza.

The hall, which is also used as the dining room, has Elizabethan or Jacobean panelling, or possibly a mixture of the two. The overmantel is probably of James I's reign and is thought to have been installed in the original Tudor house by Philip Packer's father. In the Tudor fireplace there is a fireback dated 1604, with the arms of James I. The room is furnished with splendid oak pieces: a drawer-top dining table, a Jacobean hall cupboard with inlaid panels, different types of Yorkshire and Derbyshire chairs and two or three chairs dating from Charles II with rich coverings, together with the collection of portraits which came to the house.

The kitchen is a splendid example of the huge old country-house variety. Many of the original fittings are still there, including spit racks and hooks in the beams for hanging joints and game.

Above the hall there is a room equal to it in size, known as the hall chamber, where again the walls are lined with the old panelling from the original house. This panelling, however, has original painted decoration in imitation of inlay, with an interestingly contemporary-looking criss-cross pattern of gold, black and off-white.

In the drawing room, Philip Packer abandoned his usual discretion and installed entirely new decoration, consisting of oak wainscoting with panels large enough to accommodate three-quarter-length portraits, a splendid fireplace in black marble with white veining, and an equally fine ceiling with a large oval garland of fruit and flowers in high relief, set within a rectangular framework of panels with enriched borders. The furniture consists mainly of walnut pieces of the late seventeenth and eighteenth centuries, which are almost certainly rather

with water insubstantially mirroring walls and trees, where colour counts for so much and where peacocks strut and pace on the lawns among the yews, one surrenders unreservedly to the enchanting scene.... And so in this perfect accord between art and nature one is not conscious of any anomaly in finding a Renaissance building in a medieval context.'

Interestingly, Philip Packer was most probably simply being prudent. By building his new house on the site of the old, he was able to take advantage of many of its old materials and foundations. Certainly much of the medieval panelling was reused. Old English linenfold panelling, painted Tudor panelling (the Tudors invariably painted interior wooden surfaces in bright colours), splendid Renaissance and mellow seventeenth-century panels all now line the walls where portraits of the

Above: *A portrait of Isobella Berkeley, Philip Packer's second wife, hanging above an oak inlaid chest in the hall chamber (above the dining hall).*

grander than Philip Packer could have afforded. On one side of the fireplace is an exquisite little walnut writing table, and on the other is the cabinet with its needlework portraits of Charles II and his Queen, and doors inlaid with a bold marquetry design of contrasting woods, including sycamore and ebony. Between the windows there is a mirror with borders decorated in *verre églomisé* in the French manner, probably brought over to England by the Huguenots.

On the next floor, one of the main bedrooms is also particularly interesting, not just because of its handsome Elizabethan four-poster, but because set in the windows are two beautifully painted glass sundials, presumed to have been installed by Philip Packer. Each is framed in a large diamond-shaped pane and has the motto *Lumen Umbra Dei*. There is also a fly painted on the glass, a favourite conceit in the seventeenth century.

Most of the windows on the front of the house date back to the early years of the eighteenth century – one can be precise about this because the date 'September 1713' is scratched on a pane in the dining hall and this must have been done after the installation.

All in all there is no way to fault Groombridge. It has clearly always been a much cherished house, with each new owner doing something to repair or at least maintain the structure. And it has enormous presence. Even as the setting for the acclaimed film, *The Draughtsman's Contract*, it gave such a performance that it is the house and its beautiful gardens and statuary, the strutting peacocks, the clipped yews, the harmonious ensemble of building, moat and grounds that one remembers as much as anything. Groombridge is not just quintessentially seventeenth century, but the ideal English country house. Not just a house revived, but a house that has been carefully and beautifully preserved in – and by – time itself.

Top left: *Beneath a window, an unobtrusive sign of modern times – a radiator painted to tone with the panelling.* Top right: *The magnificent marquetry cabinet in the drawing room with its needlework portraits of Charles II and his Queen. The needlework, with its figures raised in relief, is known as 'stumpwork', which was popular in the seventeenth century.*

Italian Villa

It took the Italian couturier, Gianni Versace, three years of searching to find the house he wanted. Three years is a considerable time, but Versace's persistence and patience paid off when, eventually, he made the discovery of this abandoned *fin de siècle* house, with its perfect forest backdrop, right on the shores of Lake Como. Despite its decrepitude, he knew instinctively that this was the house of his dreams.

The house seemed to have everything he wanted: peace, tranquillity, spaciousness, a romantic position, and proximity to Milan. But, like many new home-owners in the first intoxication of ownership, Versace had underestimated the time and effort that would be required to revive the property, decorate and furnish it.

A long and arduous restoration period followed. Not only had the house been abandoned for several decades, but previous owners had managed to deface, as it turned out, almost all the original decorations. Yet if Versace had not foreseen the work involved, neither had he anticipated its rewards. The process of restoration revealed just how magnificent those decorations actually were. And when all the partitions were demolished and

floors lifted, the original, generous rooms came to light, each as splendidly proportioned as a ballroom.

This once sumptuous villa was conceived and built in 1880 by an eccentric English architect and ardent nudist who went by the somewhat un-English name of Curié. Mr Curié must have had visions of grandeur, for underneath layers of filth, old paint, paper and false floors, were revealed astonishing inlaid marble floors of neo-classical designs, amazing mosaics, and cornices and mouldings of impressive proportion. Even the grounds, when cleared of years of weeds and undergrowth, revealed room for a tennis court as well as a garden.

After some research, Versace discovered that the original style of the house had been a mixture of classical Greek and Roman, strongly tinged with nineteenth-century Empire, the sort of eclecticism he loved. What it needed, now that the layers of neglect had been stripped away, was sympathetic furnishing.

Accordingly, Versace set off on a marathon chase across Europe to find the right sort of furniture, paintings and objects for the interiors he had uncovered. In Naples, for example, he discovered furniture and chan-

Left: *The villa viewed from Lake Como. Blue-grey stone and woodwork contrast with ochre-coloured walls. A double row of balustraded steps rises up to the entrance.* Above: *An heroic marble bust on a plinth strikes the right classical note. Versace tracked down treasures all across Europe to furnish the villa.*

deliers which had belonged to the Bourbons, and a series of portraits of the Edoardo Gioia family, which now line the dining-room walls. Also in Naples, he found paintings from the school of Andrea Appiani, depicting the gods, Mars, Venus, Diana and Apollo. Heroic in scale as well as subject, these now hang on the walls of the salon.

Elsewhere on his travels, Versace found splendid Empire pieces of mahogany, inlaid with bronze and gilt. These include the daybed, with carved lions' heads and inlaid with vine leaves, which he has placed in his sister's bedroom, together with a handsome writing table of the same period. In the salon is an extraordinary set of leather-covered armchairs with griffin arms and claw feet, signed by the great French cabinetmaker, Jacob. Other rare objects Versace collected include a large tapestry by Michele Cammerano, now hung in his study surrounded by a collection of military objects, uniforms, classical busts and figures, and souvenirs from past trips.

How Versace decorated the rooms was more or less dictated by the sumptuous floors, as complicated as elaborately woven carpets, which were discovered under rotting floorboards. The tawny colours and green borders of the floor in the salon, for example, inspired pale stone-painted walls, apricot curtains and large urns, overflowing with greenery, set between the long windows.

The study also has pale walls, with a greenish cast. Simple white curtains are designed not to compete with the oversized petal-patterned mosaic on the ground, warmed by a paisley-covered sofa in reds and russets. The formal geometric design on the floor of his sister's room is allied to azure-blue walls and bedcover, enlivened by a collection of gilt-framed nineteenth-century portraits of children.

All the main rooms have windows overlooking the lake, so the green-blue of Como is always in view. In return, the sight of the house from the lake, 'simple as a cube and vast as a palace' as someone described it, with its washed ochre walls and blue-grey stone and woodwork, dark shutters and double row of balustraded steps, is a memorably romantic sight.

The house looks very grand and very approachable at the same time, just like the interiors. With its calm and sense of classical order, its sun-dappled walls and pervading atmosphere of restrained grandeur, it must be a peaceful retreat from the world of high fashion.

Top left: *The salon*. Left: *Versace's study*. Top right: *An elegant reception room, used as an office*. Right: *A collection of children's portraits in Versace's sister's room*.

Belgian architect Lydia Kümel had always liked strolling, sketchbook in hand, around the various side streets of Brussels and its outskirts. One day, in the pleasantly wooded area called Uccle, just south of Brussels, wandering up a sedate street of old houses surrounded by older trees, she suddenly came across the most unexpected architectural anomaly. There, on the highest rise of the road, reared the incredible geometric steel and glass facade of a house she judged to date from the late 1920s, the golden age of Modernism, of which good Belgian examples are all too rare.

She was straight away captivated with its style, proportions, symmetry and dominating position, neglected garden and all. To this day, she says, she hardly knows what facet of the house she found, and finds, most beguiling: its Rationalist/Deco architecture, its interesting juxtaposition with its dignified nineteenth-century neighbours, or its romanticism. Paradoxically, she did find the strict rationalist style very romantic.

After this initial 'shock of the new' amongst the *ancien régime* – imagine the amazement of the neighbours in the 1920s – she often came back to see and admire the details of what she came to think of as 'her house'. Then one day in 1980 she found it was for sale. As if dictated by fate, she and her husband, Arthur Langerman, bought it and, while working on its restoration, for it needed a great deal of repair and remodelling, she started to research its provenance.

The house had been built, she discovered, in 1928, for a stockbroker who wanted a house 'in the new style'. The builder, Yvon Beaudoux, was a specialist in granite and mosaic work. According to a commercial newsletter of the time, Monsieur Beaudoux had followed the plans of a certain architect called M. Brunnenstein. Ms Kümel has never been able to find any other reference to this mysterious man, which is strange for the designer of such a powerful building, and thinks that perhaps Brunnenstein was a pseudonym.

In any case, the building was not quite finished when, in 1930, the stockbroker went bankrupt and the house was sold to a glass merchant who lived there with his family, an incredible number of crystal chandeliers, and as far as anyone knows, a good part of his glassworks as well, for some forty years. During this period, Ms Kümel says, the house underwent numerous modifications, not many of them particularly felicitous, not least the fact that the glass merchant boarded up the whole of the

Left: Lydia Kümel's Rationalist/Art Deco house in Uccle, on the outskirts of Brussels.

south side of the house, which overlooks the woodland.

In the early 1970s, the house was sold again to a professor of philosophy, who much appreciated the villa's unusual combination of Rationalism and Art Deco but did not have the money to give the house back any of its former lustre. It was a stroke of good fortune that led to its ultimate sale to the Langermans who have now restored the spirit of the original design.

'I let the house take possession of me. I tried to intervene as little as possible, either creatively or personally, with what I thought was the original concept, right up to the time when I was ready to choose the furnishings,' says Ms Kümel, who was sensitive to the house's origins but nevertheless wanted to avoid at all costs a caricature of the 1920s. 'It had also to be, after all, a house for living in the 1980s.'

To achieve this kind of delicate balance was difficult. It took months of research and more than two years of work to get the house to its present state of impressive geometric simplicity. The result is not so much a restoration as an intuitive recreation based on absolute respect for the past. Looked at now, the flat-roofed building is long, interestingly narrow and sharply angled, its exterior mainly composed of immense rectangular paned windows. The walls are faced with a rose-coloured finish called 'chromolite' which is embedded with fragments of quartz. It stands in grounds that are as deliberately restrained as the house, but terraced, hedged and planted with ground-cover in a way calculated to show off the symmetry and planes of the angular building.

Inside, the house is just as disciplined. There are

Top left: *The staircase, with its original black marble treads in* noir de Mazy, *chrome banister and irregularly paned skylight is a magnificently sculpted geometric composition.* Top right: *'The small dining room' is another exercise in sculptural geometry with a touch of hi-tech – the whole softened by the diffused light from the glass brick wall, and the cobalt glass of the table.*

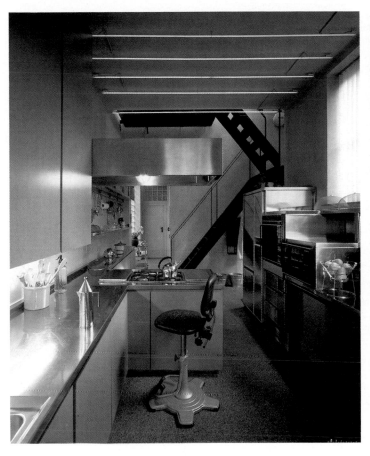 

three floors. The first is occupied by Ms Kümel's architectural studio where she works with her two colleagues. On the second floor there are reception rooms, including a music room, a large hall with the staircase rising on two sides, a dining room, another room off the kitchen known as the 'small dining room', and the kitchen itself. On the top floor there are four bedrooms, three bathrooms, two dressing rooms, a library, and a large solarium-terrace.

The original materials of the house have been conserved as much as possible. The most noticeable of these include the black Belgian marble known as *noir de Mazy* used on the staircase, the original mosaics created by Monsieur Beaudoux, the original builder, and certain of the floors, along with ebony-stained doors, and a particular sort of rubber and chrome.

The furnishings and decoration share an equal sobriety and distinction. The principally Italian furniture is a carefully chosen modern collection, displaying a use of materials that harmonizes with other built-in surfaces. The original black marble stairs, sharply angled as they are, form a magnificent geometric composition with the skylight and its irregularly sized panes. In the room known as the small dining room, walls are covered in spray paint, the floor is covered in felt, and a large panel of glass bricks keeps the geometric feel of the house, as well as providing a soft, filtered light. The table by Citterio and Nava has a top made from a sheet of cobalt glass, matching the sliding door of the buffet. The 'Spaghetti Chairs' are by Belotti and made of chrome and rubber, reflecting the building materials.

In the large dining room, the table and chairs, now

Top left: *The hi-tech kitchen was entirely designed by Lydia Kümel in a basic steel finish. Saucepans and cooking utensils are hung from butcher's hooks attached to iron rails.* Top right: *A view into the large sitting room from the terrace outside. This room is mainly furnished in a carefully chosen collection of modern Italian furniture.*

covered in a Marimekko fabric, came from another 1920s Belgium house, the villa built by Leborgne at Rhode Saint-Genese in 1929. An English silver tea service of the same period sits on the sideboard which is topped with a single sheet of black marble.

Right off the dining room is the hi-tech kitchen, with stairs leading away up to the third floor. The room was neatly designed in its entirety by Lydia Kümel. The surfaces are mainly stainless steel, with butcher's hooks, suspending the cookware, attached to iron rails.

The Music Room on the south west corner of the house is a perfect example of the 'romantic Modernism' that Lydia Kümel mentioned. Luminous walls are allied to flowing curtains of pleated silk which sweep the floor, and the long windows are neatly balanced with the 'Hill House' chairs by Charles Rennie Mackintosh, and the tall, luxuriant plants.

The large sitting room is furnished with mainly contemporary items, except for the Le Corbusier chaise-longue set by a long window leading out onto a terrace. Above it is a huge circular light set into the ceiling. There is a 'Wink' chair by Kita, a small table by Forcolini, 'Erasmo' sofas by B and B Italia, a 'Sella' seat by A. and P. Castiglioni, and a 'Bi-bi-bi' table lamp by Ingo Maurer.

The master bedroom has a bed by Paolo Priva and a 'Seconda' armchair by the Italian architect Mario Botta, while the library, with its distinguished ebony-stained shelves designed by Lydia Kümel, has a long glass-topped table inset with a broad band of sand-coloured glass. This rests on rubber cylinders which end in metal discs. There is also the classic meshed metal chair by Saarinen. Here too, long French doors open onto a splendid terrace.

The overall impression of the interior is of shades of black, grey and white, a brilliant composition of marble, steel and glass. By restoring the house sympathetically, without resorting to pastiche, Lydia Kümel has created a look that is as contemporary and fresh as it must have seemed nearly sixty years ago. It is 'a hymn', as someone wrote perceptively, 'to rigorous discipline'.

The house is also a monument to the endurance of Modernism. Its pleasing contrast of materials, clean lines, spare decoration and functional design make it a classic creation of the twentieth century.

Left: *The Music Room, which is a good example of the romantic Rationalism that so beguiled Lydia Kümel. Trailing, pleated curtains are offset by glowing wall surfaces.*

THE PERSONAL VISION

I built my soul a lordly pleasure house
Wherein at ease for aye to dwell

ALFRED, LORD TENNYSON

Texas Villa

The city of Corpus Christi is situated on one of the most beautiful stretches of shoreline in Texas, but is subject to extremes of heat and relentless humidity in summer, bitter winters and fierce annual hurricanes. Any house built right on the coveted bayside of Corpus Christi's Ocean Drive is not only at the mercy of these harsh weather conditions, but is also, necessarily, wedged between the traffic streaming along the palm-lined and immaculately lawned boulevard, and the ravishing gulf with its violent changes of mood.

Given their clients' site, a knoll rising from the bay, and that coveted state of affairs, a fairly unrestrained budget, the Californian architects, Batey and Mack, turned to a suitable archetype. Their choice, the Roman villa, the *villa suburbana*, could hardly have been more apposite, since the classic duality between the introverted public facade (onto the public highway) and the extroverted garden front (onto the bay) seemed made to order. In the architects' design, this villa theme has been reinforced through the use of classical proportions allied

to a unifying geometric order, with spectacularly beautiful materials superimposed on an elaborate foundation of piers and beams to cope with the shifting soils and tides. Sturdy exterior walls of concrete blocks under the continuous veneer of polished stone, plus bullet-proof window glass and a microzinc roof, were all chosen to withstand the worst possible climatic conditions. Andrew Batey would like to think of his clients sitting comfortably ensconced in their exquisite interiors, unperturbed by lashing hurricane-driven waves and the sight of uprooted palm trees hurtling past their toughened windows. The architects also took the opportunity to weave into this same calm geometric order such unaesthetic but practical items like transoms, ventilating exhausts, ceiling fans and high ceilings which traditionally help to modify the local climate.

On the street side, the long stretch of almost unbroken wall is clad mainly in bleached Italian travertine complemented by rosy Mexican marble veneers, punctuated only by a Honduran cypress grille inset into the

Above: *The pool, with its blue-green mosaic tiles and trembling sheet of water, appears to float surrealistically on top of the sea.* Right: *The house and pool from the sea.*

Above: *The central axis through the sitting room provides a spectacular vista of sea and sky.* Top right: *The kitchen.* Bottom right: *A bathroom. Note recurring X-motif.*

central entry pavilion. It is both refined and opulent. Hidden behind this facade is a pleasantly scaled court-yard or atrium, which not only continues the Roman theme but shields the south-facing rooms from passers-by. This space is paved and partly clad with travertine; water trickles coolly down a pair of delicately carved antique columns and spills into moats positioned at the bases of their marble pedestals. Trellises on the court-yard colonnade provide welcome shade.

From here, an eight-foot (2.5m) wide powerful central axis passes through the house and out into the sea beyond. It starts through an imposing red granite doorway, and continues into the first of three small, square, skylit spaces which both help to suffuse the interior with generous but gentle light, and create a precise transition between the outside and the interior, a necessary start to the spectacular vista through the house towards the sea and sky. The eye then continues across the gentle arc of a carefully positioned pool which appears surrealistically suspended within the bay itself.

Rough Mexican stone steps leading down to this pool are flanked with rectangular columns that suggest the remains of some noble ruin. Looking back from the bay, the water side of the house is extraordinary. Pillared porches and arbours and its rows of columns descending to, or rising from, the sea are quite lyrical.

Inside it is a rare delight to find such fine and precious materials, and such exquisite craftsmanship. The creamy Italian travertine, and the *rosa blanca cantera* and rough brown paving from Mexico are all cut precisely into twelve-inch (30cm) squares and fitted in a flawless veneer around columns, walls and floors. Beautiful cabinetwork is constructed from birch, and cypress doors have been rubbed with a transparent stain and hand-waxed to produce a soft patina. There is fine bronzework in the fireplace screens and hardware, and floorboards are edged with marble.

Furnishings are a mixture of neo-classical, as befits the house, and comfortable but gracious modern, inter-spersed with beautiful antique fragments. These make a serene composition set against the cool cream and grey-green rooms. Throughout the house, the careful modu-larity appears and reappears, in the deeply coffered ceilings, sometimes in shallow pilasters, or in travertine strips in the marble floors. The X-motif of the cypress construction across the entrance is repeated over and over again throughout the house.

Batey and Mack generally derive their inspiration from historical archetypes. But as this beautifully crafted house demonstrates, such references can be made in ways that are neither self-conscious, theatrical or trivial.

Villa Trianon

Many beautiful houses have had a sadly chequered career, their days of splendour and their days of degradation. The handsomely revamped Villa Trianon in the south of France is no exception.

It was built in 1903 on the Côte d'Azur when it was still called the Riviera, by an Italian princess when there were still Italian princesses. Its style was the kind of ultimate eclecticism which flowered at the end of the nineteenth century in Monte Carlo and Nice. That is to say it combined elements of Spanish-Moroccan, flamboyant Gothic, elaborate rococo and a good sprinkling of neo-classicism, this last particularly manifest in the Villa's name of Trianon and the pillared colonnade along the facade.

After its first glorious era when it passed from the Italian princess to the King of Laos, the house's fortunes went into decline, not to say chaos. The Communist regime who wrested power from the king also took over the Villa, using it to house visiting functionaries and visiting soldiers, some of whom were stationed as permanent armed guards among the ornamental urns on the roof terrace. The Villa, built solely for pleasure and days of wine and music, was quite unable to withstand such an occupation, and was finally left abandoned, emptied of its furnishings, its rooms ransacked, its gardens wrecked.

It was in this sorry state when its current owners found it, saw its potential, and bought it. The huge task of restoring the Villa was then entrusted to the French architect, landscape designer and decorator, Michel Alix, who spent the next two years, in conjunction with the Galerie Lear in Paris, trying to give the house back its original blithe soul.

Monsieur Alix saw his task as restoring the Villa to its original *fin de siècle* elegance using all the ease of management that the twentieth century could provide. Of the original building he only kept the exterior walls and handsome colonnade of the facade. There was not much else to preserve, and he knew that the interior, or what was left of it, had to be entirely gutted before it could be exquisitely reformed to harmonize with the magnificent proportions of the colonnade.

In all, Monsieur Alix built in eight luxuriously marbled and decorated bathrooms and two avant-garde

Above: Night view of the swimming pool with its mosaic tiles bathed in light. Right: The magnificent front entrance flanked by semi-tropical plants. Built in the heyday of the Riviera, the house suffered a decline until its present restoration by French architect, landscape designer and decorator, Michel Alix.

kitchens. He added another storey where the original roof terrace had been, and behind the colonnade he created a Roman terrace paved with white marble inset with black marble diamonds. The whiteness of the marble is accentuated by a terracotta balustrade and terracotta pots of bay trees. Frescoes depicting angels, discovered under layers of paint, were carefully restored.

Michel Alix also inserted a solarium, a bar with a long view over the sea and a billiard room. He added floors of inlaid local stone, polished like marble but easy on bare feet. He specified walls to be rubbed with wax until they attained a honeyed ochre colour associated with the colour of walls in ancient Greece. Then he decorated the walls by applying heroic Greco-Roman motifs, pilasters and mouldings.

Once the structural work was complete, the next task was to furnish the interiors. Monsieur Alix collected marble fireplaces, grand mirrors, grander paintings and beautiful fabrics. Then he set a mixture of antique

Left: *The Grand Salon with its beautiful inlaid stone floor.* Top: *Triumvirate of arches looking out over a terrace, floored in black and white marble.* Above: *The new billiard room.*

furniture, statues and objects found locally, together with comfortable upholstery, cane furniture, and contemporary pieces designed by his own studio, sometimes copied from ancient models, sometimes purely modern in concept and execution.

A grand salon, dining room, and comfortable bedrooms were all installed in their rightful place. Then, when all interiors were finished to his exacting standards, Monsieur Alix turned his attention to the garden. With the help of a specialist gardener he turned the surrounding grounds into an English park full of shady trees and flowering shrubs, complete with an immaculate swimming pool and a tennis court, the latter surfaced with the same synthetic beaten earth that Bjorn Borg used to train on for his numerous championships.

At the end of this Herculean labour, Michel Alix's vision of the house was entirely justified. He had turned the ruin back into the ideal South of France villa, grandly conceived, but as easy to live in and as easy to maintain and run, as it is possible for a house of this size to be.

Above: *A guest room. The bed was copied from an old Italian model.* Above right: *A view of a bathroom.* Right: *Futuristic basins in another bathroom.* Opposite: *The terrace.*

Wurlitzer House

For five generations the Wurlitzer family lived and worked in East Germany making clarinets. Their instruments were, and are, respected by connoisseurs and collected by museums throughout the world. But, in the 1960s, Ruth and Herbert Wurlitzer found that they could not stand living under the East German regime any longer and managed to escape across the border with their family to settle in the small West German town of Neustadt an der Aisch.

There they lived beside their new workshop, continuing to produce beautiful instruments, and continuing to make a success of their business in their new surroundings. But they dreamed of building a special house that could be specially tailored to fit all their requirements.

Eventually the Wurlitzers managed to acquire a pleasant plot of land in a former orchard, located on a southern slope just outside the centre of town. Their obvious choice of architect was their daughter, Gudrun Wurlitzer, who lives in Cologne and who they felt could build them the house they wanted.

The Wurlitzers' brief to their daughter was to build an ageless, classic house without post-modern trimmings. There should be a large music room for musical events, for up to as many as seventy people, as well as comfortable space for visiting members of their large family, which includes grandchildren. Despite the need to accommodate guests and the occasional concert, the rooms had to be the right scale for two people. Reconciling these two extremes was the challenge that faced Ms Wurlitzer.

The Wurlitzers also wanted to preserve as many trees on the site as they could, and to remain as insulated as possible from the noise of a nearby railway line which could have spoilt the otherwise peaceful aspect of their land. Mr Wurlitzer also had a particular request 'to be able to sit by a window and look out onto the road', a vantage point from which to view the world go by.

The chief disadvantages of the plot were the neighbouring houses, some of which had been built in the 1960s, just about the time the Wurlitzers had first come to the town, during West Germany's great postwar prosperity boom. But Gudrun Wurlitzer was not about to build 'another box' in order to fit in with the general ambience. She wanted to keep a distance from the road but at the same time open up the house to the south. There were also good views over the town and spectacular sunsets to the west she was keen to catch.

Then, too, her father was very sensitive to subterranean water veins and a water-diviner was called in to check the plot for the paths that Mr Wurlitzer was sure

Left: *The soaring central space of the house ends in a graceful dome. All other rooms lead off this hall.* Above: *The semi-circular house front, giving panoramic views of the neighbourhood. Local development, a railway line and ground conditions meant that siting of the house was critical.*

there were. He was right. From the water-diviner's visit they discovered that a third of the land was literally riddled with water, a factor that certainly had to be taken into account in the construction of the foundations.

With her parents' requests and the various aspects of the site in mind, Ms Wurlitzer produced a design consisting of an elegant semi-circular building set as far as possible from the southern boundary, which opens to the west, overlooking a terrace and pavilion and the town beyond. It had the requisite number of rooms, spaciously proportioned. And because of the semi-circular nature of the design, the house gave Mr Wurlitzer opportunities to study the road outside from any window he wanted.

All the while the house was being built, Ms Wurlitzer insisted that the workmen used traditional methods and materials allied to solid craftsmanship, explaining patiently her point of view and why she wanted no short cuts, supervising in the way that very few architects have the time to do. As a result, although the house cost no more than an average German one-family home, it has been built to excellent standards. Every room is beautifully detailed and beautifully finished.

Most of the interior design is created as part of the architecture. A central soaring space ending in a glass dome is the pivotal space from which all rooms lead off. There is a good sitting room and dining space as well as well-proportioned bedrooms. The kitchen is also spacious and beautifully detailed. Marble was used for the worktop and to back the shelves and a row of fitted metallic cannisters in keeping with the period atmosphere of the house.

One of the most impressive spaces is the special music room. This curved space is further accentuated by the sequence of windows, each draped floor to ceiling, making a rhythmic and dramatic punctuation. Built-in niches between pairs of curtains are used to display vases and a semi-circular raised sweep of bookshelves is set behind the comfortable seating area.

In fact, because the house does look so ageless and so much part of its surroundings, visitors are apt to congratulate the family on the superb restoration of their house, forgetting, if they ever knew, that no house existed there before. Whether this is a compliment or the reverse, Ms Wurlitzer is still trying to determine. However, she is secure in the knowledge that she has produced exactly the sort of house of which her parents had long dreamed.

Left: *The spacious music room with its long windows, emphasized by flowing drapery.*
Top right: *Beautifully detailed kitchen.* Above: *A bathroom.*

ofts, and Manhattan lofts in particular, have long been a comparatively inexpensive source of space on a grand scale. As such, they have always been heavily in demand for architects, sculptors, designers, painters or anyone who needs studio as well as living areas. Nowadays, anyone who wants space is attracted by these abandoned commercial and industrial buildings, which provide unconventional accommodation.

David and Caro Lloyd-Jacob, respectively chairman of a steel distribution company and a painter who also buys and sells antique linens and laces, bought their loft in 1982. The building in which it is located, situated conveniently midway between Grand Central Station and Greenwich Village, was built in 1912 and was one of the first fireproof 'loft' buildings in New York. It consists of twelve floors each of which has eleven-foot (3.3 m) ceilings, very thick walls and soundproof floors. Originally a factory space, its first occupants were a variety of manufacturing businesses, each with its own floor.

The Lloyd-Jacobs purchased the top floor. This had initially been used by a metal-working business, but later accommodated a company making skirts and dresses. What the Lloyd-Jacobs bought was three thousand square feet (2700 m²), completely open, with no interior walls, and huge windows providing natural light on all four sides. They also bought a rooftop building above to convert to a penthouse floor. Like all loft-dwellers, a strong reason for acquiring the space was the opportunity to have a completely free hand in its design.

To this end they decided to approach the project as a partnership, with David Lloyd-Jacob working out the distribution of space and his wife, who by her own admission was completely at a loss with this wall-less area, designing the interiors once the divisions had all been organized. They felt that the main floor should be used for general living and entertaining space, with an office for a secretary, and that the penthouse they intended to create, should be used by Mrs Lloyd-Jacob as a studio and as private quarters. They thought, too, that this upper area could become the centre of the household in the summer since it was so light and bright. Having determined the allocation of space to their final satisfaction, they commissioned an architect, Leland Taliaferro, to file plans and act as general contractor.

Left: *Part of the penthouse floor, with its magnificent Manhattan views, is devoted to a studio.* Above right: *Spiral staircase salvaged from Brighton station.* Right: *Living area.*

The Lloyd-Jacobs had always been inveterate collectors, and they put their expertise and taste to work with splendid effect on the loft. All the original hardwood floors were retained, stripped and polished. Three wood-burning stoves were installed to provide three open fires in the main living area, the library and the upstairs studio. Almost all the architectural details used were antique. The doors, which are mostly very grand, were all reclaimed from old buildings along with some splendid fanlights. The main bathtub, which is huge, came from a Vanderbilt mansion, the spiral staircase from Brighton Railway Station, the handsome columns from a Wren church in London, and the library panelling was actually from an old pharmacy in Brooklyn.

When asked how they fitted in all these disparate items so naturally – for they do indeed look as if they have been there forever – David Lloyd-Jacob said it was easy. They just created the structure around the details, rather than adding details to the structure. Even the kitchen was built around a collection of mismatched old wooden shutters bought for a few dollars apiece. At first the architect looked at them askance, but their very dissimilarity adds to the charm of the room.

Many of Caro Lloyd-Jacob's antique textiles were used to decorate the generous wall space. The colours and patterns of these fabrics, together with the oriental rugs, provide a foundation for the decoration.

Because ceilings are high and the whole area very light, large plants, and even small trees, flourish and provide a green freshness to an already delectable and airy city space. This feeling is compounded in the studio penthouse and roof terrace upstairs. The spiral stairs going up to the top level are overhung with sweet-smelling jasmine; outside, terracotta pots of plants, small trees and boxes of flowers make an oasis in the midst of the Manhattan rooftops.

Above left: *Well-furnished bathroom*. Above right: *The master bedroom*. Right: *Part of Mrs Lloyd-Jacob's fine collection of antique textiles*.

La Fabrica

*I*n one of Barcelona's grimmest and grimiest suburbs is the home and studio of Ricardo Bofill and his 'Taller de Arquitectura', arguably the most influential architectural firm in Europe. It has been variously described by the non-cognoscenti as 'a concrete tray with a castle standing in it', as 'just a building site', and even as 'an industrial ruin'.

In fact, the collection of buildings was the notorious Sant Just Desvern cement works which were responsible for enormous environmental damage. When Bofill first saw the factory over twenty years ago he recorded his impressions:

> 'Before me were enormous silos, a high chimney, four kilometers [2.5 miles] of underground galleries, machine rooms almost in working order.... If as my eyes moved rapidly over the scene, I already had a kaleidoscopic vision of another space to come, it also became apparent to me at the same time, that the cement factory embodied the new aesthetic and plastic movements developed since the First World War.'

The challenge, of course, was how to turn a horror into the sort of marvel that Bofill envisaged. 'I wanted', he said, 'to turn the ugliest of buildings situated in the most sinister of surroundings into a work of art ... I

Above: *The main entrance to Ricardo Bofill's 'La Fabrica', situated in a disused cement works*. Right: *La Fabrica is framed by a grimy Barcelona suburb.*

wanted to prove that man can transform ugliness into beauty if he has talent and will.'

Work began with dynamite and jackhammers, and continued for more than eighteen months. Bofill approached the task like a sculptor, for however brutal the tools it was precise work to try to reveal hidden forms and to accentuate certain spaces. Next came a thorough cleaning process to clear out silos completely filled with dirt, dust and cement.

The third phase involved landscaping. A softening base was needed for all those sculptural shapes, so a platform of greenery was created, with the idea that vegetation would climb up the walls from the ground and more greenery would descend from the roof. A series of terraces formed at the top of the silos were planted with grass and cypress, and linked to one another by a series of suspended bridges, also planted with grass seed.

The last phase, according to Bofill in that higher form of language that architects tend to use, was 'the annulment of functionalism' which was, of course, to transform the space from a cement factory to an architectural office and home. Bofill decided to layer the new construction with historical architectural references rather than stamp it with any vernacular architectural style. Nevertheless, there is a certain flavour of Catalonian regional tradition around. Windows, doors, stairs, false perspectives were imagined and applied on exterior walls and to certain interiors. Arches were sometimes applied with paint, sometimes incised into walls. Gothic columns and late eighteenth-century pilasters were all superimposed, albeit lightly, and mixed with other styles. Aspects of classicism, medievalism, romanticism, industrialism are all included. Staircases start and as abruptly stop in space, arcades open onto a void, pillars support nothing, all in homage to surrealism. The meticulous black and grey of the principal entrance evokes hyper-realism, while the library windows are simply like portholes on a ship.

Bofill conceived the whole immense complex as an entirely eclectic work, intentionally heterogeneous. 'The Taller is an international team', he explains, 'designing projects to be built all around the world.

Left and above: Two views of Bofill's austere but beautiful private studio which acts as library, dining room and salon. The tables are chestnut marble; the chairs are modelled on a design by Gaudi. The room reflects Bofill's belief that the beauty of a space should speak for itself, without any superficial embellishment or decoration.

La Fabrica

for conferences and concerts – music plays a strong role at La Fabrica. A huge kitchen-dining room space next door, rather like a monastery refectory, is where most of the staff take their meals, more often than not accompanied by Bach.

Ricardo Bofill's personal apartments are predictably austere. They consist of a vast studio and a more modest bedroom which have an almost religious, certainly monkish feeling, though the finishes on walls, floors, and furniture could hardly be more beautiful.

In the soaring studio which serves as library, dining room and salon, the main pieces of furniture are two chestnut marble tables, one high for dining at, one low for sitting around. At the high table are arranged a set of chairs modelled on a design by Gaudi who, after Michelangelo, is Bofill's greatest inspiration. Either side of the low table are, respectively, a sofa and upholstered stools covered in leather. A few more chairs are backed up to a side wall and books are simply propped on a shelf with no titles showing. The fireplace is a simple rectangular hole and the floor is exquisitely inlaid. There are no pictures, no objects, no flowers. For Bofill, the beauty of an interior lies in its proportion and detail.

In the bedroom the mattress is hardly raised above the floor. A simple marble top behind it acts as a night table. To balance it, a marble bath is sited at the opposite end of the room underneath one of the rows of elegantly arched windows that both studio and bedroom share. Both rooms open out from these windows onto arcaded terraces planted with cypresses and creepers.

Bofill says that he has the impression that he is living within the walls of a closed universe – as, of course, he more or less is. He adds that it is the only place where he can really work and really think. 'La Fabrica is like a free-thinking lay convent dedicated to work. Life unfolds in a continuous manner with little difference between work time and free time.'

Bofill's output is prodigious. With the Taller, he has designed schemes for sites all over the world, including France, Holland, Spain, Algeria, the Middle East and the United States, collecting many architectural awards in the process. Although some of his best-known and most controversial work are his large housing developments in France, many people seem to think that La Fabrica will turn out to be his greatest accomplishment.

Their freedom of expression must in no way be constrained or directed.' He wanted there to be contradictions (as in the perfectly designed windows placed next to gaping holes in the facade) to symbolize the state of aesthetic tension that he likes to exist among his staff.

The old silos are now full of rooms, their outside walls perforated with Gothicized twin-arched windows. The disused hoppers have been formed into vague sculptural shapes: 'partly Baroque, partly Moorish' as one architectural magazine succinctly described them. In one huge ground-floor space in the old factory building, light filters in through the massive concrete as if through the stone and marble of a cathedral, which indeed is the name the space has earned. It serves as an exhibition area, a room

Above: *The notorious Sant Just Desvern cement works included huge silos which Bofill retained and on the third floor of each he created offices. The rounded walls have been incorporated into his design as these details show.* Right: *Bofill's bedroom displays the same monastic simplicity, with a low bed and sunken marble bath in front of arched windows.*

Any reader of the works of D.H. Lawrence or Emile Zola will be familiar with the scarring inevitably inflicted by coal mines on often beautiful countryside, it being one of the sad ironies of nature that some of the finest seams are to be found in the finest landscapes. The indignation caused by this rape of nature was at first very bitter, but, as in the case of most outcries over visual horrors, ameliorated over the years to a dull, pragmatic apathy.

Amongst most people, that is. There were and still are people willing to fight with all the strength they have to conserve the land or, perhaps better, rehabilitate it after it has given up its riches.

Gerald and Mary Cookson had a reputation for making beautiful homes and extraordinary gardens, and for caring about both people and land. They had owned a house in the east of England, in Suffolk, which gave enormous pleasure to anyone who visited it. They had tended to every detail of decorating and renovating the main house and its offshoots – for the Cooksons can never resist converting every building in their ken.

Then, in the 1970s, as part of an inherited estate, Gerald Cookson was left a farm property in a coal-mining area in what was once a beautiful part of the Pennines. Dramatically sited 800 feet (240m) up in the hills, overlooking open country, the house had been tenanted by sheep farmers. Since the Coal Board said they no longer needed to mine in the area, the Cooksons decided it would be a challenge to take up the farm and its house, reclaim the land and try to make it beautiful again.

The Cooksons' Suffolk friends were sad, if not entirely surprised, to see them go, and expected great things of the new venture. But when they eventually saw the place, a little square stone farmhouse set bleakly on a hill surrounded by a few outbuildings, a collection of slag heaps, and hardly a tree in sight, even the most ardent of the Cooksons' admirers were not quite so optimistic. The scale of the task that lay ahead seemed immense and utterly daunting.

As it turned out, however, any misgivings proved totally unfounded. After ten years or so of the most diligent work the house, garden, land and outbuildings have blossomed to an unprecedented degree. What the Cooksons have coaxed from the savaged land is a near miracle. What is more, they have created a group of

Left: *The tawny-hued dining room with walls
covered in hessian, handsome
eighteenth-century furnishings and late
eighteenth-century Irish wake table.*

harmonious buildings surrounded by soft landscaping that looks as if it has always existed there, undisturbed by humans, let alone coal mines, for centuries.

Predictably, the Cooksons had just as difficult a struggle with the Coal Board as with the intemperate northern climate and the harsh prevailing wind. Although the Board was generous with rehabilitation grants for shrubs, tree planting, wind-breaks, the removal of slag and so on, and undeniably had the best will in the world, it was also beset by the weight of bureaucracy.

Nevertheless, the Cooksons persisted and gradually the house and its outbuildings were renovated and expanded. They knocked down walls, built new ones, extended outwards, put up hothouses and installed a splendid new kitchen. The dairy side of the house was rationalized to include laundry, dirt and gun rooms en route to the garage. The front entrance was changed, and comfortable, generous bathrooms were added as well as a new drawing room. All of the mantelpieces, including the handsome white marble surround in the

Above: *The inner sitting-hall with its warm colouring – so necessary in the north – has a deeply comfortable ambience. This room, which is used more than any other by the Cooksons, is the pivotal space around which the layout of the house was conceived.*

central hall, were also additions. The ruins of an old gin gang (a perfectly round stone barn) was turned into a guest house with a couple of romantically decorated guest bedrooms, a bathroom, studio, small kitchen and a games room *cum* sitting room, which is also an excellent room for parties.

The whole house now works like a rather grand country house, yet on a scale more suitable to the late twentieth century. Despite the transformation it remains, on the outside at least, very much a northern farmhouse, if a considerably prettier one than before.

When a visitor steps inside the house for the first time, nothing (except visiting a Cookson house before) could prepare them for the shock of surprise, the change from the quiet rurality of the stone exterior to the distinction of the furnishings, and the enveloping colour and warmth inside. Mary Cookson, who is as good a landscape painter as she is a gardener and hostess, did all the painted finishes throughout the house herself, not by following any particular method or set of instructions but

*Above: A corner of the drawing room where the shelves of old books, the pastoral paintings, log fire
and easy chair combine to create the atmosphere of an old English library. The handsome
white marble fireplace was an addition, as were all the other mantelpieces in the house.*

Top: *A view of the kitchen*. Above: *The garden room lined with long mirrored panels*.

just concentrating on the effects she wanted to achieve and working it all out by trial and error. The result is inspirational. The colours of surfaces and furnishings were chosen to create a warm, cosy atmosphere to counteract the bleak effect of the northern light. And in the garden room, the walls are lined with long, mirrored panels, as are the backs of the shutters, for maximum reflection of daylight.

To some extent, climate has also dictated the way the house is arranged. The internal layout of the house has been totally reordered so that the house is planned as a square around a central space, a layout which is excellent for preserving warmth in the harsh northern winters and cool in summers. A small entrance hall now opens onto a very much larger, warm terracotta central hall with its own fireplace and comfortably chintzed sitting area, which is used a great deal being situated as it is in the core of the house. The dining room leading off to one side of this sitting-hall is a beautiful tawny room covered in hessian, with grey-blue woodwork and spectacular eighteenth-century furniture, Persian rugs and early paintings. This, in turn, opens into the kitchen with its handsome and practical quarry-tiled floor, custom-built wood units and combination of Aga stove – that mainstay of the English country house – and electric hob. Mary Cookson painted the scene above the stove, just as she designed the kitchen for her own needs. At one end of the immensely long room is an old dresser (hutch); at the other, a casual eating area, leading into a comfortable library, or den.

On the other side of the sitting-hall is the long, more formal drawing room. From this you reach Gerald Cookson's study *cum* farm office with suitably battered leather chairs and a handsome desk. Two staircases lead up to the bedroom floor which is again extremely comfortable and well-detailed. Every room has its own writing desk, lighting is good for reading, there are comfortable armchairs, and adjoining bathrooms have generous tiled ledges all around on which to rest glasses, soap, powder and bath essences. The Cooksons' own bedroom is especially spacious with a handsome four-poster bed, beautiful rugs and a fresh, beautifully detailed green and white scheme. It is a delightfully relaxed, enchanting room.

The warm colours, the splendid furniture, paintings, rugs and objects, and the plethora of plants make this house the very model of country living. That the Cooksons managed to turn the unpromising material with which they started, into the enjoyable and aesthetic experience that they created, is a tribute to both vision and hardiness.

Above: *The spacious master bedroom with its four-poster bed, green and white colour scheme and oriental rugs. The rich textures of the fabrics enhance the room's country character.*

Old Malt House

Maltings, malt houses and mill houses are among the few types of industrial buildings to be found in rural areas. When converted, they provide the same enviable space as their urban counterparts, but with incomparably better views. This particular malt house, situated on the banks of the Kennet and Avon Canal, is a Grade II listed building dating from 1850 and sits surrounded by 'unforgettable, unforgotten river smell' as Rupert Brooke would have it, with moorhens and coots among the reeds, and swans, kingfishers and narrow boats slipping silently through the water.

The building was lying empty when interior designer Tony Heaton discovered it on a casual visit to Bath. Since, in spite of its proximity to the water's edge, it was only a brisk walk to Bath Station and the London train, and since he was looking for an unusual space with character, he bought it.

Viewed from the other side of the canal, the building is dwarfed beside the old Malsters warehouse next door, but it looks charming with its hipped roof and arched windows, its facade half-hidden by creeper and trees. The only clue to its past function is the tall boarded chimney. Inside, however, the soaring space is extraordinary and it is difficult now to believe that when Mr Heaton first bought it, it had already been converted to a mass of partitioned and 'modernized' rooms. These were immediately demolished. Simplicity is what Mr Heaton wanted, which is hardly surprising as most of his work consists of creating decidedly elaborate interiors for Middle Eastern clients.

After renovation the Old Malt House now consists of three levels. The ground floor is on a level with the canal itself and you climb up a flight of steps from a small stone courtyard to reach the lawn and the waterside, or, conversely, down the flight of steps to enter the house.

In some ways, this first space is like a great cool cathedral crypt, with its graceful stone vaulting and deep arched window embrasures. The floor is of heavy quarry tiles in variegated tones of sepia, ochre and indigo, each tile being minutely pierced in an interestingly formal pattern. Originally, these same tiles were on the floor above, forming the base on which the barley was fermented. The barley would be brought in from the harvest, spread over the floor and left to germinate in warmth and humidity, until the grain had almost completely fermented from starch to sugar and turned to malt. At that stage the furnace in the crypt-like floor below was stoked, the fierce heat rising through the pierced holes in the tiles to kill and dry the grain. Gradually the great bed of barley would roast until it was judged to have reached the peak of perfection and could be shipped to the local brewers.

Now that all that aromatic cycle is in the past, the former furnace level, now so cool, is Mr Heaton's general

Left: *Although the Old Malt House is dwarfed by warehouses on either side, its interior space is very generous.* Above: *The dramatic half-platform supported on a single pillar.*

living area, part kitchen larder (in what was once the furnace), part living room, part occasional spare bedroom. It is furnished very fittingly. The worktop in the kitchen is made of solid slabs of maple supported on Bath stone end walls, the same Bath stone that used to be shipped in great slabs on to barges and transported up the canal outside. Chairs, refectory tables and cupboards are simple scrubbed pine.

The first floor, apart from similarly deeply arched windows, is quite different in feeling and structure. Everything is either white or pale wood. A single timber pillar and impressive fan of joists support a partly cantilevered second floor above, and very little has been allowed to interrupt this dramatic sight. A guest shower room is just visible above a short flight of steps, a white towelling curtain looped back behind the arched entrance to hide the plumbing. An open fire and bread oven cut across a corner, enclosed by the old iron doors of the furnace. The bare pale wood floor has been toned right down with many applications of household bleach and on this level, too, there is very little furniture: a large white sofa and coffee table made from a solid chunk of English elm; kelim cushions to break up the white; a pine mirror and blanket chest set with blue and white china; an old table left behind by the previous owner supporting a glass bowl of daisies.

Behind the sofa, a cluster of plants half conceals a green-painted cast-iron spiral staircase leading up to Tony Heaton's bedroom and bathroom on the third, and topmost floor. This balcony room on the half-suspended central deck lies directly under a skylight framed by black joists and white boarding. Cane chairs and table are painted *eau de nil*, a touch of colour amid all the careful pallor and, as the sun glints on the water of the canal below, a faint ripple of light is reflected on the ceiling. The lines of the original building give the rooms great interest with their strange shapes and unusual features. They act as the main decorative device and create a unique atmosphere.

From here there are only muffled sounds to be heard from the city, and the echo of those convenient trains. Only the abbey bells interrupt the still air with their clear ring of sound. Otherwise there are really only water noises: the splash of a water fowl, the murmur of small boys fishing. By stripping the building back to its industrial past, Mr Heaton has created a calm interior well in tune with this simple, peaceful setting.

Top left: *The sleeping balcony with its integral bathroom*. Below: *The kitchen*.

Above: *The first floor living area. Here the airy space with its dramatic fanned-out ceiling joists and massive support pillar is kept mainly white and rather nautical.*

Paris Apartment

Anne-Marie Beretta is a fashion designer known for her extreme elegance. She holds rigorous discipline very dear – cut, structure and an instinctive choice of appropriate material are of supreme importance, and everything must be reduced to its purest simplicity. As if echoing the art historian Mario Praz's dictum that 'the house is an extension of the ego', this discipline is just as apparent in the decoration of her beautiful ground floor apartment in *le quartier chic*, the sixteenth *arrondissement* of Paris.

Long, spacious rooms with impressively high ceilings are simply but exquisitely furnished, and open for the most part, onto a luxuriantly green garden. They look, with their splendid cornices, pilasters, plaster friezes, arches and handsome panelling, about as architecturally distinguished as rooms in an apartment building can be. One envies Madame Beretta her luck in finding such a space, until you hear of the work that she and designer Colombe Stevens put in to achieve all this aesthetic perfection. At this point the envy turns to admiration for the patient dedication they needed to remove false ceilings, extraneous details and muddy colours to reveal the purity beneath.

'I wanted', she said, 'an apartment that had some osmosis with the garden. Therefore for the interiors I chose some materials that are generally used for exteriors.' In the hall this means a floor of polished stone;

in the salon and study, the kind of large slabs of travertine used to face facades, or clad columns. Walls to go with these distinguished floors are a beautiful, clear, restrained colour somewhere between a grey and a beige, though not that somewhat dead colour commonly referred to as 'greige'.

An intensely visual person, Madame Beretta says she has been much influenced by Japan, particularly by the colours of its landscape – the near-black earth, the deep green of the vegetation – and the fact that art seems everywhere, made by and for everyone. A window with one object precisely placed on its sill, a tiny garden glimpsed at the end of a street, is worth all the poetry in the world to her. And she has tried to create the same purity which so entranced her in Japan, in her own home.

The furniture she prefers is almost always designed by architects because she finds it to be invariably both thoughtful and functional, not just made for decoration. Her hall appears enormous; its length magnified by a completely mirrored wall which reflects a pair of polychrome copies of seventeenth-century angels, and two turn-of-the-century armchairs set side by side, designed by Kolomon Moser for the Wiener Werkstätte. Nothing else. Madame Beretta explains that she knows how it is much more difficult to keep a space empty than to fill it, so she is always cautious about buying objects or

Left: *The spacious hall with its mirrored wall.* Above left: *Screen brought back from Japan by Madame Beretta.* Above right: *Japanese screen and Corbusier chairs in the study.*

147

furniture. For instance, she says, she is looking for a particular lustre light. It might take her twenty years to find exactly what she has in mind, but this does not matter; she is not one to believe that there is an art in compromise. And, in any case, the monasticity of the entrance suits her perfectly. Conversely, she does not mind getting rid of possessions, changing them for something even better, as long as they do not go too far away from her, preferably to family and friends, so that she can still see them from time to time.

In the study, which is the place where Anne-Marie Beretta does most of her thinking and designing, the romantic garden outside is reflected time and again in the mirrored panels of the walls and even, in part, on the ceiling. Her work table, lit by a Pipistrelli lamp by the Italian, Gae Aulenti, is veneered in pale walnut and dates from the 1930s. It was actually a flea-market find. Her work chair looks like a resplendent maharajah's ivory throne but is actually veneered in a patchwork of wood resembling marquetry. On either side of the fireplace is a first edition Le Corbusier chair, grouped on

Above: *Sottsass armchairs in the salon.*
Right: *A longer view of the salon.*

Above: *The dining room looks over a dreary courtyard, so Madame Beretta painted it a dark grey and installed opaque windows. The lacquered table was designed by Ruhlman.*

one side with a Le Corbusier *chaise-longue*, another Japanese screen and a long narrow glass vase.

In the salon there is a conspicuous lack of a sofa since Madame Beretta does not like to sink down when seated: 'Comfort, yes. But not softness.' Instead, she chose four armchairs by Ettore Sottsass for the simplicity of their line and grouped them at right angles round a glass and chrome table. The table is placed over a bowl of foliage and white blooms and surrounded by an arrangement of pillows covered in an ecru linen. The transparency of the table is repeated in the perspex (plexiglass) globe sculpture by Marta Pan and in the thick glass top of the starkly handsome table by Pierre Chareau on which she has placed a sculpture by Marino Marini. On the mantelpiece, the sole object is a crystal vase kept full of arum lilies. To either side are two 1920s lamps by Prinz, found in different antique shops. Since she often likes to combine both masculine and feminine elements in her clothes, she thinks of these lamps, she says, as masculine and feminine elements too. The black *torchère* as the male, the white as his bride. Both are complemented by the curved vase-like lamp on the side table. Two final but disparate touches of exoticism are at the other end of the room: the old brass telescope reflected in the arched mirror over the fireplace, and a sumptuous gold-leaf screen brought back from Kyoto on her first visit to Japan.

Since the dining room faces north over a less than distinguished courtyard, Madame Beretta took the opportunity to install opaque window glass and paint the walls a very deep grey. The spectacular black lacquer conference table (for the room is also used as a workroom and for showing audio-visual material) was designed by Ruhlman in the 1920s and made by the French furniture company Jansen in 1960. The chairs are contemporary designs by the Italian architect, Mario Botta. Two etiolated halogen lamps by Gilles Derain are silhouetted against the window and flank a small table by Pierre Chareau. The room, so sombre and dignified by day, comes to life at night with spotlights and neon.

Predictably, the kitchen is as exquisitely monochrome as the rest of the apartment. The best part of the room, Madame Beretta thinks, is the square of glass bricks cut in two by the marble column (which disguises utilitarian pipes and flues). 'It's as handsome as a modern painting.' Worktops and the eating counter, where she takes quick meals with her husband and son, are faced with a beautiful, practical pale grey marble to match the floor.

The whole apartment is as practical as it is aesthetic. And it could hardly be a better illustration of Mies van der Rohe's famous three words: 'Less is more'.

Above: *Two views of the kitchen with its crisp monochromatic design.*

Converted Factory

Ray Gill, a young Australian architect, lives and works in his own visionary conversion of a derelict turn-of-the-century inner-city factory in Sydney. Much as Ricardo Bofill was inspired by the vast, grimy cement works in Barcelona, so Gill, in his own way and to a different scale, was moved to try his hand and creative mind at turning the old iron springs factory into an open-air living and working environment. His model, however, was not the sort of kaleidoscopic historical overview of architectural styles that Bofill implanted to such effect in his cement factory. Gill happened to admire the pavilion approach to open housing that he had seen in Bali, complete with proliferating garden areas and retaining courtyard walls, a style which he felt could well be adapted to the configuration of his old factory and to Sydney's benign and sunny climate.

Gill's first thoughtful move was to start work on the now luxuriant garden, not particularly easy in an area completely covered in concrete. But, undeterred, he built the necessary retaining walls, and shipped in fifty tons of good soil, had it heaved on to the appropriate plots, and began planting, choosing plants and shrubs that would need the absolute minimum of maintenance. Only when all his greenery and trees were established and a good overhead watering system installed, did he turn to the removal of the decrepit roof and the planning of the living-working space.

He was determined to preserve as much as possible of the original structure and to use only materials current at the turn of the century which would weather well and be, like the garden, maintenance-free. This resulted in the happy mixture of Western red cedar trellis, shutters, blinds and lattice-work, etched glass, brick and hardwood floors, and corrugated tin roofs. Original red brick walls were bagged with mortar inside and out, sometimes with a hint of red oxide to give the quality of unrendered masonry.

Before the renovation began, the floors in the main living area were covered in bitumen and some seven layers of old linoleum, punctuated here and there by various holes to accommodate machinery that had to protrude to the lower level. All these many layers had to be stripped down and the holes filled in with dowels of

Left: Trellised verandah with curved corrugated roof leading to the bedroom wing behind an arched doorway. Above: Once an iron springs factory, the building's conversion was based on the pavilion style of Balinese housing. An original stairway leads to the living area.

hardwood to match the wood that was finally discovered underneath. When they were eventually smartened up, many of these floors were stained green. All the dilapidated window frames had to be replaced, as did much of the glass simply because it was beyond cleaning.

Gill carefully segregated his working and living spaces, although he fitted in an extra guest-room off the ground floor workshop, and an exceedingly pretty but tiny guest retreat off the main courtyard with a ladder leading up to a bunk bed. His own living quarters were sited on the top floor. Here an open-plan living-dining room and kitchen area is overlooked by a sleeping loft, with a brilliant blue ceiling and matching chair, and vivid mosquito netting wrapped around the bed. Ray Gill's own bedroom is separated from the rest of his living space by a cool-looking trellised verandah, roofed with curved corrugated iron painted green, and approached through a handsome arched door.

Furnishings are spare and idiosyncratic, which suits the space very well. Lockers salvaged from an old tobacco factory do very well for storage in one of the work areas. An old unused mirrored door is hung on a wall as a decorative object. Kitchen chairs are painted a spanking white. And all around is the lush foliage, the varying greens repeated in the stained wood of floors and stairs and some of the walls, contrasting with the old brick and lattice-work of cedar wood.

The use of materials is particularly joyous. Ray Gill has so orchestrated it that rough of brick contrasts with smooth of polished wood. The crisp geometric design of the latticed wood used for inner balconies and outer terraces makes, together with all the foliage, a spectacularly horticultural antidote to the otherwise industrial nature of the place; the delicacy of etched glass and curved windows is played off against the massive thickness of the walls, painted iron girders and brick piers; just as the almost medieval arches of the bedroom verandah, and the repeating curve of the roof (has corrugated iron ever looked better?) serve as an antidote to the long parallel lines of the wooden bench.

It is a serene oasis. In fact, it is all so peaceful and green it seems entirely removed from city bustle until you catch glimpses of distinctly urban views through chinks in the shutters. But then the prevailing green surrounds one again like a cocoon. If more derelict city structures could be revived and renovated so cleverly and with such obvious delight in materials, what a promising outlook there would be.

Top left: *Courtyard floor shows a delight in different textures.* Top right: *Brightly-coloured sleeping loft.* Right: *Sitting room, with expanse of polished wood floor. Many of the factory's floors were covered in bitumen and layers of linoleum, and needed extensive restoration.*

THE SPIRIT OF PLACE

*No house should ever be **on** any hill or on anything.*
*It should be **of** the hill, belonging to it,*
so hill and house could live together
each the happier for the other.

FRANK LLOYD WRIGHT

*O*ne of the most interesting exercises for modern architects is how to make use of historical inspiration in its right physical context, or when it seems mannerly to do so, without sacrificing contemporary thought, creativity and technique. In short, how to be tactful aesthetically without sacrificing originality.

Hugh Newell Jacobsen, the Washington-based architect with an increasingly large international practice, excels at this, a point that obviously comes across in various articles about his work. When the owners of this Pennsylvania house were in the process of deciding who to commission to build their home, they made an extensive study of current work before they made their final choice.

Mr Jacobsen, for his part, was delighted with his new clients' choice of site, a kind of park at the end of a one-and-a-half mile (2.5 km) cul-de-sac studded with different manifestations of the American Dream: splendid replicas of Tudor, Georgian and Dutch Colonial homes,

Left: *The facade of the house with correct 1750s detailing in the clapboard cladding, and exposed foundation.* Above: *The witty, telescoped side with mirror edging.*

each with their own immaculately landscaped grounds. 'At the end of all this', he describes, 'was a perfect green carpet before a towering wall of white pines, which obviously dictated a tall house.'

But the problem was one of tact. In the first place, Mr Jacobsen discovered, none of the long-term residents had ever imagined that the pleasant land at the end of their road could ever be built on. And if that was not shock enough, his clients wanted a simple, modern, indoor-outdoor house which would hardly blend in with the neighbours.

Mr Jacobsen's initial reaction was to look around at the best of the local vernacular, which happened to be the telescopic eighteenth-century buildings that the Amish built. These 'telescope' houses were purely practical – their form was the result of a sequence of additions made as families expanded. His second thought was to make an abstraction of that tradition for his clients' facade (which would please the neighbours) with all the modernity, light and space that his clients expected, built in behind. His final witty and, as it turned out, brilliant solution was to design no less than seven units, descending in height and narrowing in width in regular increments of two feet (60cm) on each side. At each reduction, he planned on filling the left-over wall and roof space with special insulated glass which was reflective on the outside for day-time privacy indoors, with normal see-through glass inside to admit natural light and different glimpses of the grass and trees outside. All this culminated at the tall west gable which he suggested should be clad from top to bottom in reflective glass to mirror the trees and sky.

'No doubt', he said, 'if the Amish had had access to materials like reflective and insulated glass they would have made good use of them. But they didn't, so they couldn't. But what I was able to do, in fact, was build a glass house with respect to the Amish.'

When he showed his model and sketches to his clients, the husband, a successful general contractor, studied the plan with care, then announced that he wanted to build it. He saw it as a challenge – structurally – with windows at every corner where support posts would normally be.

His wife was not so sanguine. 'I don't want to live in a joke,' she said, 'I don't mind an amusing house, but not

Top left: *Looking up from the hall to second and third storeys.* Bottom left: *Third floor landing with insulating glass outlining the eaves.* Right: *A view of the large sitting room.*

a joke.' But her husband was gently adamant: 'I'd like to build it.' Then he added, 'But if you are not happy with it when it is finished, we'll sell it.'

In the event, she was very happy and so is almost everyone who comes to the house, struck each time by the almost Magritte impression that the house gives: a modern design that is not *quite* an Amish house, a Shaker farm, a clever restoration . . . and all those slithers of mirror reflecting the greenery so wonderfully. Best of all, the neighbours did not complain.

It is hardly surprising. Hugh Newell Jacobsen's achievement was to adhere rigorously to a Pennsylvania style of 1750 in the proportions, the pitch of the floor, in the configurations and dimensions of the small-paned windows, in the narrow clapboards, the raised panel front door, the exposed foundation at the right height and in the correct size of brick – slightly larger than today's norm. All of this is perfect 1750s, beautifully detailed, adroitly managed.

In contrast, the interiors are spare, tranquil, beautifully designed light and airy spaces which are certainly the best of the 1980s. The plan of the house works in such a way that each of the seven 'telescoped' units has its own use, unfolding one from the next. Rooms flow into one another literally, and flow visually to the outside through sliding glass doors onto a terrace, and through the long slithers of glass in all the corners.

It is not so much disorientating as re-orientating and invigorating. The space seems to flow upwards, too: to the roof in the case of the dining room, kitchen and spacious entry hall, where a spiral stair ascends to the second and third storeys, revealing the interior workings of the house rather like a sectional drawing.

Internal materials are as carefully chosen as those of the outside. Steps and a wide passageway, leading from the living room to foyer to library, are paved with Pennsylvania bluestone. Walls are meticulously painted, and everywhere are these panes of glass, reflections, shafts of sunlight, tantalizing glimpses of the green and blue outside. At night, privacy is maintained by uplights concealed under trees which reflect off the mirror-glass.

The living room is outstanding. Although extremely large, with outdoor views in all directions, it is nevertheless comfortable, even intimate in feeling, an effect gained from the different treatments of the glass walls, the choice of furniture and its arrangement.

The delighted clients are enthusiastic about a total change of lifestyle. For many years they had lived and raised a family in a conventional suburban house with an increasing number of possessions. In this house, restraint comes naturally. No one is tempted to add anything extraneous. The house has a tremendous sense of innate order, yet paradoxically that very order and restraint seems to encourage a kind of spontaneity.

Left: *The living room is full of sunlight and there are views in every direction.* Top left: *The calm, collected kitchen with its own small, glass-walled eating bay.* Top right: *The luxury of an exercise room which seems almost open air. The inside/outside feeling that the clients specified has been successfully achieved at no cost to the formality.*

St Michael's Mount

St Michael's Mount, a castle built on top of a rocky outcrop off Marazion, on the west coast of Cornwall, has been the home of the St Levan family since 1659, and must be one of the wildest, most romantic homes in Britain. It is certainly one of the most isolated residential buildings in Europe.

The Mount is regularly cut off from the mainland by the tide. To reach it visitors can pick their way over the stony causeway when the tide is out, or take a boat across when the tide is high. In winter, they use a 'duck', an amphibious lorry which can negotiate high waves. Once on land, there is a clamber up a rocky path through the beautiful gardens planted with tropical trees and shrubs, to the castle's entrance. Stores and luggage are transported by underground railway cut through the rock. At night the castle is cut off, since it is too dangerous to take boats out in the dark.

The present Lord St Levan who, with his wife, has lived in the castle for the last decade, is a direct descendant of the Colonel John St Aubyn who first bought the castle from the state in the seventeenth century. Under their stewardship, the castle has retained its great historical flavour and imposing presence, while losing none of the charm that has made it such a beguiling family home for generations.

Historically, the Mount itself has an impressive pedigree. From the twelfth century the Mount was garrisoned to protect the surrounding coast from marauders. It was this garrison which first signalled the approach of the Spanish Armada. As Lord Macaulay wrote, some 300 years later:

> *From swift to East and swift to West,*
> *the ghastly war flame spread*
> *High on St Michael's Mount it shone,*
> *it shone on Beachy Head.*

But the history of the Mount goes back centuries earlier than that. Since 495 AD when St Michael was supposed to have appeared to some fishermen, the island, culminating in a craggy summit called St Michael's Chair, has been a place of pilgrimage. Edward the Confessor established a Benedictine abbey on the Mount, and Richard, Duke of Normandy built a sanctuary on the

Above: St Michael's Mount seen across Mount's Bay from Marazion, the small town on the mainland. Right: A closer view of the castle. The stone path leads up to the entrance through beautifully planted craggy slopes. The building dates back to the twelfth century and was for many centuries a garrison until it was bought by Colonel John St Aubyn in 1659.

rock on which St Michael was said to have appeared. During the Middle Ages, its reputation for miraculous cures was known throughout Europe. Today, the Mount still attracts pilgrims – some of them newly married couples. According to local folklore, whichever spouse first sits on St Michael's Chair will have the upper hand in the marriage.

Pursuing the secular theme, the island was also supposed to be the home of the giant that Jack killed. The legend has it that a giant called Cormoran lived on the Mount, making forays to the mainland to steal cattle. His supremacy went unchecked until he was challenged and killed by a brave Cornish boy called Jack. Interestingly, when alterations were being made to the church in 1906, an underground chamber was discovered in which lay the skeleton of a man well over seven feet (2m) tall.

It was Colonel St Aubyn who domesticated the island in the seventeenth century and some of the rooms in the castle have barely changed from that time. The Royal Coat of Arms celebrating the Restoration of King Charles II, who lodged at the Mount on his way to the Scilly Isles, still hangs over the fireplace in what was once the monks' refectory. The room is now called Chevy Chase because

of its splendid plaster frieze of hunting scenes. The chairs are modelled on the chairs originally used by the monks, but the room is too far from the kitchen to be used for dining on a daily basis.

In the eighteenth century, Sir John St Aubyn, the third Baronet, made some alterations, knocking the original Benedictine Lady Chapel into two beautiful drawing rooms decorated with fine rococo Gothic plaster-work. One is now known as the Blue Drawing Room. In it hangs a family portrait by Thomas Gainsborough, and there are still cushions upholstered in the original 1740s fabric on some of the chairs.

The small drawing room leading off the larger room has, like the room next door, a wide tower window overlooking the sea. There is also a rare landscape painting by John Opie. Opie happened to be a local painter, the son of a Cornish carpenter, and was described by Sir Joshua Reynolds, no amateur himself, as Caravaggio and Velasquez rolled into one. History, as it happened, did not seem to concur, but Opie's work remains beautiful.

One of the most attractive bedrooms is called the Princess Room because Princess Alexandra, later wife to

Top left: *The main hall with one of the many flights of stairs:* Top right: *The vestibule to the Blue Drawing Room, Strawberry Hill Gothic arches are echoed in the back of the chair.*
Right: *The Chevy Chase Room, so called because of the hunting frieze around the room. It used to be the monastery refectory – chairs are a copy of the old monks' chairs.*

Edward VII, stayed there while her husband went on a visit to the Scilly Isles, obviously a favourite place for kings to visit. The four-poster bed was discovered in a farmhouse on the mainland by Lord St Levan's father, and bought because the frieze around the top matched the frieze in the Chevy Chase room. No one knows, however, whether this was the bed in which the princess actually slept.

Despite the battering Atlantic gales, the endless flights of stairs, and the disconcertingly different levels – one of the problems about living on top of a rock – the St Levans find the castle a wonderful place to live, with its constantly shifting views of sea and sky and its gardens full of rare plants. Given such a degree of exposure, it may seem unusual for the cultivation to be so lush. But the castle also benefits from the effects of the warm Gulf Stream which runs all around the Mount, making it possible to grow botanical specimens that cannot be grown anywhere else in Great Britain.

Although the castle looks immense from the mainland, and especially imposing from the bottom of the Mount, it is actually quite manageable with some ten bedrooms, five sitting rooms and a chapel, apart from the usual kitchen and bathrooms. The St Levans use them all, even the ones shown to the National Trust visitors (the castle was given to the Trust in 1954 with the proviso that the family could go on living there for a thousand years if need be). They feel quite strongly that unless they continue to use the whole castle as their home, it could easily lose its charm and become cold and formal, something it is most certainly not at the moment.

There is a nice juxtaposition between the impregnable-looking external granite walls, and the light and airy Strawberry Hill Gothic of the eighteenth-century rooms inside. The solidity outside, the thickness of the towers, turns to near fantasy indoors with the sprightly arches repeated in the Chippendale chair backs, and there is also something very touching about the superimposed signs of twentieth-century living, the comfortable sofas and armchairs, the pretty chintzes, the polished wood floors, the patterned curtains, the crisp white mouldings, all set against such ancient grandeur.

St Michael's Mount has to be one of the most dreamlike of all homes in the world. It has all the appeal of a fairytale castle.

Left: *One of the sitting rooms. The comfortable English interior is a total contrast to the ruggedness outside.* Top right: *Gothic window overlooking the sea.* Above: *Vestibule.*

Chelsea Studio

At the turn of the century a studio in Chelsea, London's Bohemian quarter, was considered rather raffish and romantic, with its overtones of George du Maurier's *Trilby* and the heady environment in the *salons*, the artistic and literary circles of the time. The opportunity of living in Augustus John's old studio, the home of one of the pre-eminent and most sociable painters of the time, was not to be turned down by anyone at all sensible to the memories of the atmosphere of those years, the heyday of Edwardiana and the 'Naughty Nineties'.

The lady who did buy it was certainly cognisant of that atmosphere, even though by the time she first came to see the studio it had been modernized, and had lost some of its original character. But at first sight she was captivated, seeing the chance not only to recreate something of its old feeling, but also to reinterpret a good deal of her own past as well. In an odd way, the studio reminded her of the atmosphere of a much-loved hunting lodge in Iran – Persia in this context – which had been in her family for years and was now lost to her.

The idea of combining the style of an old Persian hunting lodge with a turn-of-the-century Chelsea studio is not so very strange. There was a great deal of Middle Eastern exoticism about late nineteenth-century design, with its plethora of oriental rugs and cushions, and pattern juxtaposed with pattern, just as there was much

Above: *A collection of Persian tiles in the hall.*
Right: *View of the studio through the*
spiral staircase going up to the gallery. The large
carpet on the floor is a 'tent' rug.

of the Far East and India in the interiors of a hundred years earlier. The new owner of the studio wanted to emphasize this 'vagabond' style, as she called it, with all its nomadic influences.

Interestingly, at first sight, the present decoration of the studio space with what seems immense numbers of cushions, pillows, rugs, hangings and curios of all sorts does give the feeling of a lavish Edwardian studio, but once you look more closely you notice scripts from the Koran, mythological birds, Persian paintings and artefacts which give a specifically Persian atmosphere, exotically foreign to the London streets outside. Antique textiles are thrown over side tables and divans in a *degagé* way, as well as hung on walls.

The natural light is wonderful by day, pouring in through the double-height windows and rooflights, dazzling the rich colours and textures with shafts of sun. Light at night is mostly provided by candles in antique candelabra, supplemented with well-controlled spots (a

legacy from the previous owners) focused only on specific objects and paintings.

Except for the addition of a spiral staircase, Augustus John's studio had not been much altered structurally since it was first built. Appropriately enough, the commission came about when John met a Dutch architect in a local pub. The architect, fired with enthusiasm, expressed a desire to design and build a 'continental' studio for the painter. John was obviously taken by the idea and the result was entirely successful. Not only did the studio become the centre of Augustus John's dazzling circle, it also functioned admirably as a workplace. Today, sitters still recall how marvellous the light was there.

After Augustus John's day, the studio provided a happy environment for another famous resident. The doyenne of British comedy and stage musicals, Gracie Fields, made it her London home for a while.

With such a fortuitous design, the only alteration the

Left: *View of the studio looking up to the gallery and through to the anteroom.* Above left: *The stained glass doors propped against the window were from a Persian greenhouse.* Above right: *A corner of the gallery with musical instruments and one of the mythological birds with human heads said to bring good luck.*

new owner had to make was to construct a little anteroom off the studio space, complete with a fireplace, to provide an intimate area away from the main room. Since she loves to entertain on a large scale, but informally, the way the space is now divided is ideal for her. So, too, are the colours, for the mellowed terracotta of the walls makes a warm linking background for the rich patterns displayed by her collection of rugs, cushions and textiles.

The exotica starts in the hall with a collection of Persian tiles displayed against a bright yellow wall. The top panels show tribal women wearing traditional dress, often as many as four skirts at one time, all with different designs. Chanel apparently was so fascinated by these textiles that she borrowed their motifs for her own fabrics. (One of these tribal skirts is used to cover the coffee table in the main studio.) In one hall corner opposite a fireplace, a large statue of a Turk stands on a plinth in front of a series of panels said to depict scenes from the Crimean War, reading a book of Chaucer which the owner whimsically placed in his hands.

In the vast main room, one wall is almost entirely taken up with a huge window, against which is propped two stained glass doors from a Persian greenhouse 'where old men and young girls are supposed to retire to meditate in peace and write poetry'. Another pair of ancient doors, this time made of wood, is hung on a wall. The centrepiece of the room however, is a large 150-year-old 'tent' rug which used to be thrown down on the ground outside the old family home for community gatherings. Since it has been in her family for so long the owner believes it is a 'blessed' rug and brings good luck. It is surrounded and in some cases covered by many other kelims and rugs, and woven Turkoman and Farohan cushion covers. One large cushion is covered with a true 'carpet bag', the kind in which nomads tied up their bed rolls and possessions.

On the walls, which are almost as layered with prints and patterns as the floor, are scripts from the Koran, paintings on glass, and a large Sufi pattern for tiles with a large script, which in translation reads: 'I have crossed seven rivers – God is almighty'. More framed calligraphy is hung on the gallery walls at the top of the spiral stairs, along with a large portrait, some mythological birds with human heads (also believed to be symbols of good luck), a mother-of-pearl inlaid gun box, a series of urns, musical intruments, and more colourful pillows.

This is a house of collections, but not in the sterile, considered sense. Everything on display has a personal meaning; little is shut away behind glass, and the naive and spontaneous pieces are prized as much as those that are rare and valuable.

Furniture in the studio and gallery include a long refectory table used for display, plenty of side tables for entertaining, inlaid chests, two enormous double-seat basket chairs and, in the gallery, a mirrored table. In the anteroom, which is small, intimate and full of memorabilia, the dominant feature is the fireplace. This has an unusual wrought-iron firescreen with candle-holders at either side decorated with masks. Above the fireplace is a glazed sixteenth-century medallion.

The area immediately beneath the gallery acts as the dining room. Here, the chairs around the circular table are made of ebony and come from India, while a pair of doors from the 1920s have been made into a cabinet.

The whole place is an extraordinary paean to a wonderfully exotic and comfortable eclecticism. There are few tangible things that remain of the studio's previous occupants. On her first visit, the present owner noticed a *récamier*, where Augustus John used to pose his models, and admired some Delft tiles in a bathroom which Gracie Fields had installed. These were lost in the shuffle of ownership, but what could not be taken away was the Bohemian spirit of the place.

Left: *Ebony chairs from India surround the dining table.* Top right: *A statue of a Turk stands on a plinth before a series of panels depicting the Crimean War.* Right: *Another view of the hall panels.*

Sydney Beach House

This house is one of those buildings that seems to positively exult in its surroundings. It balances easily and gracefully, almost at cloud level, right over the sea and sand on one side, and among the branches of cliff-top trees on the other. The surf pounds and breaks right under the windows, and the interesting glass and concrete structure appears to soar into the clear Australian sky.

But the house is more than just an aesthetic triumph in a spectacular location. It is also a triumph of endeavour and perseverence against a series of daunting difficulties. The site, though extraordinarily beautiful, was not exactly easy to manage. The plot had been on the market for two years before the owner bought it, basically because no one else could see how they could possibly build a house on such a steep gradient.

Fortunately, the new owner also happened to be a builder with both imagination and energy, who disliked taking 'no' for an answer. He chose a local Sydney architect, Stan Symonds, to execute the design, took him to the site on Palm Beach, north of Sydney, and gave him the shortest possible brief. 'The site is impossible,' he said. 'But I want level access and plenty of space. And it's got to be different. Apart from that, go for your life and I'll build it.'

The results were so gratifying that several years later the owner still maintains that Stan Symonds is the greatest unsung architect in Australia. Even so, the site was not the only problem. The city council threw up every possible objection to the design, demanding every sort of certificate, the owner remembers, except perhaps one guaranteeing air-worthiness! Then there was a public protest about the possible despoliation of the Palm Beach ridgeline. But finally they were left to get on with the building unhampered.

'It took four months to even get out of the ground,' the owner recalls. And little wonder. Four extremely thick concrete piers had to be embedded twenty feet (6 m) below the ground into solid rock, which required singular skill and tenacity. On top of these was placed an enormous concrete slab reinforced with steel bars, on which the house now rests.

The amazingly angled windows, reaching twenty feet (6 m) from the floor to the ceiling, are another tribute to the skill and perseverance of the owner. When the house was all up and quite finished structurally, this glazing provided the last stumbling block. Every supplier and every glass expert that the owner consulted said there was no way that they could supply or make such windows. If they did not refuse the job outright, they

Above: View of the house seen from the drive. The master bedroom is on the lower level,
the living room and wrap-around deck on the top.
Right: The front of the house overlooking the magnificent expanse of Palm Beach.
Virtually nothing is allowed to impede the view.

quoted absurdly high prices, citing the impossibility of the angles and the danger of the work. When it looked as if no one was willing to meet the challenge themselves, the owner took matters into his own hands, found a super-toughened tinted glass designed for heavy wind loading, had it cut to size, built some special scaffolding, and installed all the glass himself.

The detailing of the house, the way it all works, is just as carefully conceived and executed. The whole house is ducted for both air-conditioning and under-floor heating. In fact, the concrete slab of the base becomes one great radiator in winter if needed, but it hardly ever is because the house is so well built it really regulates the tempera ture itself. Since it faces north-east it is cooled by the

north-east breezes in summer, while in winter when the wind direction alters, the glass walls catch the sun and retain the warmth. Other thoughtful details include the fact that the wide, curving balustrade on the deck holds concealed lighting, and the guard rail beneath is made of laminated glass so that nothing interferes with the view of the sea.

All the interior spaces are comfortable, but spare and minimal in deference to the outstanding view. In the kitchen, for example, there is no splashback behind the sink to interfere with the sea and sky. Thoughtful as in everything, the owner-builder created an extra wide worktop with additional depth behind the sink to cope with splashes, and to enable the glass to extend right

Opposite above: *A corner of the master bedroom.* Opposite left: *The kitchen taps stand out like small pieces of sculpture against the horizon.* Opposite right: *The sand-coloured kitchen counters.* Above left: *The sauna off the master bathroom.* Above right: *The bathroom, with red basin for colour.*

down to counter height, so that standing at the sink is like standing behind the wheel of a boat. The counter itself is formed from thirty layers of fibreglass, in the same pale terracotta colour as the sand below. It was moulded *in situ* without seams, and if it ever scratches can easily be rebuffed. So that absolutely nothing can distract from the outside, the only furniture in the room are the stools by the countertop, and all the normal kitchen clutter and impedimenta is kept behind closed doors, out of sight.

The main bedroom on the lower level has a bed and chairs and a masterly view over the trees to the sea and sky; and its bathroom, all in white Corian (a synthetic marble) and fibreglass, with its spa bath and adjoining sauna, seems to float right over the Pacific. The living room-dining room on the upper level opens to the deck on two sides and is furnished with soft Italian sofas and other neutral-coloured Italian pieces inside, and comfortable cane outside. There are no paintings (not that there are any solid walls anyway) and no incidental objects, for the owners feel that it would be wrong to compete in any way with the seascape all around, and the spectacular, sculptural soaring angles and levels of the house within.

There are, however, plants to reflect and reinforce the colour provided by the branches and greenery outside.

In addition, there are three more bedrooms for the family, another bathroom, a study, and a mezzanine room downstairs. The latter was originally built as a billiard room, but is now mainly used as a family room and an indoor place for the children to play.

From the outside, the house has a futuristic appearance; inside, too, everything is as sleek as a space capsule. But this is no 'high-tech' superimposition, with cheerfully exposed ducts and pipework, and industrially inspired impedimenta. Here the design and technology are one; a feat of engineering.

This is entirely appropriate, since without modern structural techniques and modern materials, it would probably have been impossible to build anything at all on such a precarious site. The streamlining and beautifully integrated and engineered services call to mind one of Le Corbusier's famous sayings, that a house is 'a machine for living'. But the technology here is more than merely functional, it has been put to work for an aesthetic purpose as well. 'My wife wanted a house with a view,' says the owner. 'We gave her the ultimate.'

Above left: *The deck on the upper level. It starts among the trees one side, finishing among the clouds on the other.* Above right: *The view along Palm Beach from the mezzanine family room.* Right: *The living room and the wrap-around deck, with concealed lighting in the balustrade.*

*L*a *H*uerta de la *P*alma

Marbella in southern Spain is blessed with a splendid climate, a beautiful position on the Mediterranean, and a lively social life which attracts people from all over the world. It is accordingly very popular as a resort, and land there is difficult and expensive to purchase.

The owners of this intensely coloured and interesting villa were fortunate enough to have acquired an orchard as part of a family estate, situated just above the town, and with its own plentiful supply of spring water – a particular luxury given the general dryness of the area. But apart from the water, the flowers, the trees and the background range of mountains, there were the delectable views: the Mediterranean to the south, the Sierra Bianca to the north, and on clear days in winter even the coast of North Africa. There was also, of course, the position of the property, which was conveniently near to both sea and town centre.

This site, with all its advantages, was the ideal place for a resort home. Its owners commissioned the Swiss architect, J.-L. Vik of Zurich, to design a villa capable of accommodating a family with grown-up children and up to ten house guests, yet providing as much privacy as possible for all. They also wanted room to entertain on a larger scale, and the villa had to be as easy to maintain as it was easy to entertain in.

In terms of design, the clients wanted a happy mixture between an ideal classical Venetian villa and the local Moorish-Andalusian tradition, yet modern and comfortable, with a good-looking pool near the house. In essence, what the clients were after was a house in 'post-modernist' style.

Post-modernism, the term that has come to be applied to a certain recent strand of design, has as many detractors as advocates. Advocates argue that, in the wake of the brutality of much of 'modern' architecture, what is now needed is a sympathetic, approachable reworking of past styles, human in scale and interpretation. Detractors, on the other hand, object to this backward-thinking approach, and particularly take issue with some of the means and methods post-modernists have adopted to achieve their ends – flimsy applied decoration, unhappy stylistic clashes, visual anomalies.

This villa, however, with all its fine materials and harmonious planning, would not provide any critic of post-modernism with ammunition. Monsieur Vik's solution was spectacular, both in format and colour. The

Left: *The post-modernist portico, leading into the marble entrance hall.* Top: *The house seen from the bottom of the garden.* Above: *The stunning pool.*

exterior of the house is washed a deep lilac pink with deeper blueberry architraves around the front door and windows: Hispanic style, with classical references.

The interior, which displays strong Palladian affinities, is just as breathtaking as the facade. The front door, flanked by two free-standing columns, leads into a cool marbled entrance hall. From here, the house soars up to a vaulted glass roof, with galleried floors on either side of a long and elegant, beautifully planted and watered central atrium. Plants cascade down from these balconied galleries like water from a series of fountains to the real fountain below, and doors lead off each gallery floor as from a narrow street or arcade.

This design, despite its crisp look of modernity, is actually firmly rooted in the classical tradition. For centuries it has been adopted as a way of keeping interiors cool in hot climates and is as common in the building styles of India and Africa as southern Europe.

Leading off the inlaid marble patio on the ground floor is a formidable collection of rooms: a small living room, a grand living room, a formal dining room, an everyday dining room, a large kitchen and the servants' quarters.

On the next floor there are two extremely comfortable suites of sitting room, bedroom and bathroom, four more bedrooms with two bathrooms, quite apart from two further rooms in the tower above the entrance, and a large basement and wine cellar. It is all modern in feeling and yet familiarly classical and Mediterranean at the same time, an exotic and fanciful mixture which is perfectly attuned to a holiday villa.

Most of the rooms have marble floors, often inlaid with contrasting types, and the emphasis is, above all, on coolness. Filmy white curtains and covers, and white seating keep it all very summer-like, with the plants and the occasional important piece of furniture standing out like sculpture against the prevailing whiteness.

The surrounding gardens, formed from part of the orchard, are uniquely connected to the house by the colours of the plants. But the real focus of attention is the swimming pool to the side of the house, a postmodernist triumph with its pale fuchsia walls, punctuated by pillars, tumbling flowers, and striking black and white upholstered seating. Village houses and the mountains beyond are reflected in the clear water. Here it is truly *la vie en rose* on summer days.

Top left: *The highly modern and well-planned kitchen with its central island.* Left: *The airy, informal dining room.* Right: *The spectacular central atrium.*

Mediterranean Watchtower

The idea of making a vacation house out of an ancient watchtower perched high over the Mediterranean, with nothing but wonderful craggy Tuscan coast and sky around you, would certainly be a dream for most people in love with peace and tranquillity. And it was a dream Signora Giovanna Ralli of Rome found irresistible when she first came across this late sixteenth-century tower, built by King Philip II of Spain during the Spanish occupation of Italy.

It had originally been conceived as one of three such towers, part of the fortification system the Spanish set up to guarantee a safe landing for their citizens and to guard against invasion by marauding Arabians. When Signora Ralli first bought the tower there was just one basic room covered by a terrace, with a look-out post that reared straight up from the centre like a forefinger held to the wind. The surrounding wall enclosed a narrow flight of stone steps that led to a drawbridge and then to the front door. All around was the typical bushy vegetation of that part of the Mediterranean coast, blue-green mountains, a great bowl of sky and deep blue sea.

Entranced – and patient, as anyone has to be with the vision to restore any ancient structure – she entrusted the renovation and conversion of the tower to architects Roberto Einaudi and Massimo Lorenzetti, with instructions to somehow fit sleeping accommodation, a living room, kitchen, eating area and two bathrooms into the space, but to change nothing, or at least very little, of the basic structure. She herself wanted to work on the furnishing of the interiors, and determined to keep them to bare essentials so that there would be little to distract from the attraction of the massive structure and the incredible azure views from the deeply recessed window-openings.

The architects were ingenious and set about looking for corners, odd spaces, or any hollowing out they could do which would result in spaces for new rooms. They managed, for instance, to squeeze in a long narrow kitchen and eating space by digging out the area below the steps and drawbridge. An oval-shaped cistern, which was found in the foundations, was turned into one of two bathrooms, with a bedroom next door. And a two-bed loft was provided by building a mezzanine structure in the large living room, with metal beams and pine boards.

In spite of the added rooms, the structure really does seem untouched, still in its ancient form. Even the bathroom in the cistern, with its thoroughly contemporary

Right: *The old sixteenth-century Tuscan watchtower, built by the Spanish.*

fittings, seems totally at home and not at all alien.

Furnishings, too, are as minimal as Signora Ralli had envisioned when she was first planning the rooms in her head. And, although modern, these are entirely in keeping with the atmosphere of the tower. For example, in the living room, the fireplace has been completed with a long plain pine mantel and the simplest possible base in white painted brick and stone incorporating appropriate holes for wood storage. The cane sofa by Vittorio Bonacina is backed by a simple table by Piero de Martini for Cassina with two stick-back chairs and the white table by the chimney is by Zanotta. Altogether, there is an air of deep tranquillity – a perfect holiday home.

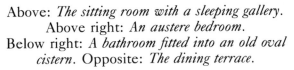

Above: *The sitting room with a sleeping gallery.*
Above right: *An austere bedroom.*
Below right: *A bathroom fitted into an old oval cistern.* Opposite: *The dining terrace.*

The Blackhoe

For some people, living on a boat is infinitely satisfying, even if the boat happens to be an old Thames sewage barge moored among the flotilla of houseboats on London's Chelsea Embankment. There is, of course, the perpetually lulling lapping of the water, except when the tide is right out; the luminous light that rises from the river at dawn, at sunrise; the ghostly shapes to be seen through the river mists; quite apart from the pleasant contrast of living at the heart of a bustling capital city but in what is an unusual riverside environment.

One of the anomalies of the Chelsea Embankment, however, is that the houseboats often seem more house than boat, and perhaps more gypsy caravan than either, with their punk colours, their hanging baskets of geraniums and lobelia, their lines of flapping washing and their rakish carriage lamps, fixed askew. This old barge, the Blackhoe, is altogether different. Its owner, a young Swedish executive who works mostly in New York, has had it de-rusted, spiffed up, neatened, smartened, its interior totally redesigned by Julian Powell-Tuck and Mark Lintott, partners in the architectural and design consultancy, Powell-Tuck, Connor and Orefelt.

The owner wanted everything white; fittings and furnishings kept to a minimum; an expansive feeling, and total purity. But it takes a lot of time, a lot of care, and generally, a lot of underpinnings to achieve the sort of pared-down look, the kind of deceptive simplicity that also functions well and comfortably.

In this case, the underpinnings consisted of steel girders, custom-built portholes, and custom-built curved cupboards and units. There are also great sweeps of curving soundproof glass to provide a panoramic view of the river and shoreline, and to cut out the unfortunate and far from romantic roar of traffic rumbling along the Embankment *en route* to the motorways.

As Julian Powell-Tuck has now redesigned the barge, the principal living area consists of one very large general living space, with a galley kitchen built into the bow in an extremely clever curve. Because of the grand sweep of soundproof glass all around this space, the visitor is aware of shapes rising up one side of the boat and disappearing off screen as it were, on the other side, but since all outside sound is muffled it is more like the golden days of the silent movies than the *cinéma verité* we know today.

Left: *The studio-living room is now a spare but elegant space, with a fireplace and concealed bookcases behind the panelling. The opened hatch in the foreground is immediately above the bed in the master bedroom.*
Above: *The barge, moored on the Chelsea Embankment.*

Furnishings are kept to a spare minimum, just a pair of large comfortable sofas by the French doors leading from the deck, a couple of black 1930s curved chairs, a dining table *cum* desk and an upright chair. Proper windows have severe little roller shades, and there are no objects on display other than a simple carved urn standing on a box which opens up to reveal a staircase down to the lower deck. Even the bookshelves are hidden behind the fireplace panel. The doors at either side of the chimney wall, which open into the kitchen-galley, have been set slightly at an angle, again to give a sense of perspective.

The only real decoration is the subtle introduction of abstract areas of grey, painted in strategic places on the walls by artist Sally Greaves-Lord, to give a feeling of shadow and depth to the otherwise general whiteness. On the floor of the living room are rugs in a quiet grey and white design – to most people an understated and hardly obtrusive touch. The owner, however, finds them unnecessary in this simple, minimal environment and will probably remove them completely to reveal a gleaming expanse of polished floorboard.

Below deck, the space is again agreeably generous. The same gentle grey shadings on the walls down here not only relieve the ubiquitous white, but lead the eye in a specific direction, through the two guest rooms with the friendly conversation hatch built into their party wall, past the den or television room, along a narrow corridor flanked by a surprisingly roomy shower room and bathroom, and on through quite grand double doors to the master bedroom. Here, with the hatch to the deck open on a summer's night you can lie and look up at the stars, while behind the bed a door inset into the panelling provides a direct escape onto the deck.

The whole boat is a masterpiece of clever planning and dovetailing, with not an extraneous detail in sight to detract from the general effect of spaciousness. Moored next to the usual hotch-potch of Bohemian river life the Blackhoe looks positively elegant, shipshape and trim. Who would have thought that this economically planned, thoroughly comfortable, white and gleaming boat could possibly have started off life as a sewage barge? It does not seem possible that this splendid riverside home could have ever had such lowly antecedents.

Top left: *In the living room, angled doors either side of the fireplace increase the long perspective and open into the galley kitchen.* Top right: *The main bathroom with a sauna leading off to the right.* Right: *The master bedroom, with a painting by Sally Greaves-Lord.*

Manhattan Apartment

When Robert Stern, one of the current leaders of American architecture, as well as one of its foremost apologists, was approached to design this Manhattan apartment, he found it a particularly interesting project. Some years before, he had designed another apartment with almost exactly the same configuration of space, in a strictly minimalist mode. He now found it an exciting challenge to reconsider a problem for which he had already found one solution.

For this apartment, he had the general idea of making a great classical design with meticulous attention to detail, to enhance the stunning space and make the most of the light and view from all sides. He wanted to design rooms of extraordinary quality using a free interpretation of classical details.

His clients, for their part, said they had knowingly bought something of a wreck, comprising just two huge rooms on two floors, and little else. They chose the building because of its convenient location on Fifth Avenue, its spectacular views over Central Park and in all other directions, and for its extraordinary spaces and high ceilings. They chose Mr Stern because they much

admired other work he had done and his general sense of style and quality; when they met him, they found they liked him, too. The brief his clients gave to Mr Stern was quite specific. They wanted a handsome sitting room which would take advantage of the fact that there were windows all around, a good dining room, a small office, a large kitchen, a back staircase, four bedrooms and bathrooms, and a special area for their five children to play games, listen to music, or watch television and videos. Then they moved into a hotel with all five children and waited, and waited.

It took a good six months to work out all the complicated plans and details on the drawing board, and because both floors of their duplex had to be completely gutted and then rebuilt, it took another two years to put it all together in its new incarnation. Work of the quality that was expected, after all, is not done in a day. But it was well worth the wait.

The apartment not only looks luxurious, it is luxurious. Right from the start, the vaulted entry vestibule with the magnificent free interpretation of classical details (cornices, pillars, pilasters, mouldings and arches)

Left: *The beautiful marble staircase.* Above: *The entry vestibule with its classical mouldings, vaulted ceiling and sophisticated lighting.*

creates the mood that Mr Stern was seeking to achieve. All the details are built in solid plaster, and are repeated and reinterpreted through the various spaces.

Robert Stern was particularly concerned to bring an awareness of the park into the sitting room. The trouble about being high up, he explains, is that you cannot actually see those fabled views when you are sitting down. Accordingly, he decided to treat the space somewhat like a stage set. By designing a spectacularly turned marble staircase coming right down into the sitting room, with different views from the windows as you walked up and down, he managed to make Central Park seem like a great green lawn below, and an integral part of one's experience of the space.

Another of the tests Mr Stern set himself was to not only produce the most up-to-date services he could – highly sophisticated lighting, heating and air-conditioning – but to disguise the most annoying features of those technologies, like wiring, holes in the ceiling, hardware, pipes and radiators. To this end he tried very hard to create recessed lighting where he could and to engineer other ways of disguising light sources; and to conceal all other manifestations of technology behind mouldings, elegant grilles, or pillars, or to make them in some way fit in with the general classical image.

Above: *New furniture is designed to fit in with the overall concept.* Right: *A view into the sitting room.*

Casa Palapas

There can be very few people who have not dreamed of living in a tropical paradise. Half facing the Caribbean, half the Atlantic, the Dominican Republic with its jungle terrain, cascading waterfalls crashing into deep pools, mountains, beaches, spectacular climate, and ever-present sense of history is one of the most interesting of the Caribbean countries.

The Republic occupies the eastern two-thirds of the island of Hispaniola, Haiti occupying the western third. Its capital, Santo Domingo, is the site of the first European settlement in the New World. Christopher Columbus, who gave the island its name, landed on the north coast in 1492. The Spanish subsequently established a colony on the east side, while the French occupied the west. Despite a troubled history and various attempts by Haiti to take over the entire island, the Dominican Republic remains Spanish to the core and relatively unspoiled.

Even now, communication between the various points of the island is difficult. Travelling from place to place is best by small plane, and the absence of road traffic or railways certainly makes for an idyllic peace. The sun shines and shines, a refreshing breeze ruffles the scented air, the foliage is lush and studded with bright tropical blooms.

It *is* a kind of earthly paradise, at least as far as Dru and Minnie Montagu, an English couple, are concerned. Some years ago, when the Montagus were staying a mile or so up the coast on a golfing holiday, they came across a small headland on the Atlantic side of the island. Wholly beguiled, they decided to start a home there, and bought the site, even though it was entirely overgrown by a thick tangle of brambles. They were convinced that they could transform it into a kind of Garden of Eden.

Although the traditional architecture of that part of the world is either sixteenth-century Spanish colonial, or white-painted clapboard with cut-out wooden tracery around eaves and verandahs, the Montagus decided they wanted something more exotic. They had seen and admired houses by the Yacqui Mexican Indian architect, Marco Aldaco, particularly a house he had designed for an uncle in Acapulco. They very much liked his use of the *palapa*, the Mexican term for a more or less circular, conically roofed building, thatched in dried palms, which is supported by pillars at regular intervals. The gaps between pillars are filled in to make a back wall and the rest is open to the air. *Palapas* are so seductively cool

Opposite: *The Atlantic Ocean seen from the* gran palapa. Top: *An aerial view of Casa Palapas.*
Centre: *A view of one of the buildings.* Above: *The* gran palapa.

and airy they make perfect tropical sitting rooms, or 'sitting-out' rooms as they really are.

The Montagus went ahead and commissioned Senor Aldaco to build their house for them, but they were not quite prepared for his idiosyncratic way of working, with none of the preliminary plans or other of the types of documentation, drawings and so on that clients have become used to getting from their architects or decorators. Nor were they prepared for the way Senor Aldaco *feels* his way over a property, communing with its every aspect, checking the sun's path over the vegetation, taking note of the directions of the prevailing winds, imagining the positions of windows that would frame a particular vista or vignette.

Once Aldaco has sufficiently absorbed every aspect of the land and every one of his clients' requirements into his memory, he stalks around, fiercely concentrating, unsmiling and silent, until inspiration begins to fuse all these separate facets together into a tangible idea. He then dashes back to the site where he draws out the shapes of various buildings directly onto the earth, using sticks as markers, arm spans and shoulder heights as measurements for doors and windows. Only then, to everyone's relief, does he make a perspective drawing. Finally the clients can see what he is proposing, and feel that there are at least some specific instructions for builders to follow.

Aldaco's solution for the Montagus was a large main house for the family, where they could sleep, bathe, cook and eat. This, he decided, should be loosely connected by shady terraces and palm-vaulted walkways to their own large *gran palapa*, for general sitting and lounging around. Down a winding walkway leading from the main buildings, he envisaged a pool behind cascades of hibiscus and bougainvillaea. Beyond the pool, he planned a terrace to be shaded by a pergola covered in white-flowering vines, which he thought should be used for lunches, and beyond that again, via a series of exotic flower beds, he decided on a guest house with two bedrooms, bathrooms, its own kitchen and *palapa*.

All this has now miraculously come to pass, right down to the flowering bushes and vines, and perfectly detailed thatch and supporting pillars for the *palapas*; a miracle of ease and refinement, all achieved without any of the usual designing paraphernalia and mounds of paperwork. Given the relaxed venue, it only seems appropriate.

Furniture is hardly a problem in an Aldaco house. He designs a good deal of furniture and fittings along with the original structure so that they seem to grow out of the buildings quite naturally. Bedheads are sculpted right into the wall behind beds, which are concrete platforms covered in mattresses. Dressing tables and bedside tables, shelves and closets are all built into the walls. Baths, sunk into or placed on platforms, grow out of the floor. Long wide banquettes, formed of concrete with comfortable seat and back cushions, are used for sofas. More sculpted concrete makes side tables. And Senor Aldaco himself adds decorative dados, friezes, murals, and any other extramural touches that he may feel are required, such as brightly painted window frames to set off a magnificent view.

Chunky solid mahogany tables were made by local craftsmen and most of the generous cane chairs which are everywhere, along with cane stools and side tables,

Left: *View into the* gran palapa *with its intricate thatch and capacious, comfortable seating. Much of the cane furniture was made locally by a Chinese craftsman.*
Above: *A neatly-designed bar area.*

were made by a Chinese craftsman living on the island. Other leather and cane chairs were made in Mexico.

A good many of the soft and lighter furnishings and accessories also came from Mexico: thick white ribbed cotton for the sofas and embroidered cushions or pillows and area rugs. Big glass jars, silvered inside like thermos flasks, are used as lamp bases. Blue and white ceramic tiles decorate the dining tables. The attractively washed-out pinks and blues of the pillows propped around the bottoms of pillars in the *gran palapa*, and piled on the floor in other parts of the room, were formerly brightly, even garishly, embroidered and coloured Mexican dresses, unpicked and recycled as pillow covers, bought to fade like jeans in the steady Dominican sun.

Then, too, there are nicely exotic touches with colour. The floor of the *gran palapa* is painted palest pink, walls in other rooms are washed in palest terracotta or sky blues. Dark, heavy wood is juxtaposed with light cane and thatch. A window frame might be painted bright blue against a white wall.

In this complex, with its indoor-outdoor life, the landscaping is just as important as the buildings. Because of the balmy climate and endless supply of water, trees, shrubs, creepers and lawns, which would take twenty years or so to grow and mature in most of Europe and America, have burgeoned and propagated in a fraction of that time under the unwavering blue sky. And among the flowers and foliage, surrounded by gently lapping sea, butterflies flutter, hummingbirds swoop gracefully, and one is enchanted by the other rare birds, egrets and pelicans. In fact, the Montagus considered calling their home 'Pelican Point' until they learned that the islanders would translate their far from prison-like surroundings into 'Alcatraz'. Instead, they christened it Casa Palapas after its distinctive collection of buildings.

The Montagus live in this blissful place for seven months of the year, taking off every now and again in their private plane – they have an airstrip not many minutes from the house – for a day or a weekend in Mexico or the United States. Viewed from the air, the meandering complex of buildings, surrounded by lush green flowering foliage, edged by azure sea, topped by the bluest of skies, looks exactly what it is – a tropical paradise and a perfect location for a dream house.

Above left: *The main bathroom, with its window wide open to sea and sky.* Above right: *A recessed bedhead, sculpted into the terracotta pink wall, is seen through a mirror.* Right: *A charming bedroom, with four-poster canopy bed, painted dado and cotton rug.*

Left: *The lunch terrace, strung with white blossom,
the table laid with blue-and-white
Mexican pottery. The concrete benches scattered with
comfortable pillows are typical of the
general seating.* Above: *A view into the dining
room: three other arches lead into the
kitchen, terrace and sitting room.*

Index

Acknowledgments

The publisher thanks the following photographers and organizations for their kind permission to reproduce the photographs in this book:

1–5 David Massey; **6 left** Derry Moore; **6 right** Richard Paul; **7 left** Casa Vogue/Tim Street-Porter; **7 right** Camera Press; **8** Zefa Picture Library; **9** Fritz von der Schulenberg; **10 left** Derry Moore; **10 right** Agence Top/J N Reichel; **11** Hutchinson Library/Dr Nigel Smith; **12 left** Richard Bryant/Arcaid; **12 right** Robert Estall; **13** Impact Photos/Julian Calder; **14 above** Hutchinson Library/Bernard Régent; **14 below** World of Interiors/James Mortimer; **15 left** Hutchinson Library/John Downman; **15 right** Hutchinson Library/Bernard Régent; **16** Rex Features/Denis Cameron; **17** Ezra Stoller © ESTO; **18–23** Derry Moore; **24–29** Marie Holstein – courtesy House & Garden © 1983 by The Condé Nast Publications Inc; **30–35** Vogue Living/Rodney Wiedland; **36–39** The World of Interiors/Tim Beddow; **40–45** Jacques Primois; **46–51** Gilles de Chabaneix/Marie-Claude Dumoulin/Elle; **52–55** EWA/Michael Dunne; **56–61** George Mott/Conran Octopus (exterior design Mark Hampton, field consultant Ronald Jacquemin); **62–69** Richard Paul; **70–73** EWA/Jerry Tubby; **74–79** Sudhir Kasliwal; **80–85** Langdon Clay – courtesy House & Garden © 1985 by The Condé Nast Publications Inc; **86–89** Derry Moore; **90–93** George Mott/Conran Octopus (Oak Alley Foundation); **94–99** Peter Baistow; **100–103** Conran Octopus; **104–109** Casa Vogue/Santi Caleca; **110–115** Casa Vogue/Tim Street-Porter; **116–121** Top Agence/Pascal Hinous; **122–125** Camera Press; **126–129** Simon Brown/Conran Octopus; **130–133** Top Agence/Pascal Hinous; **134–135** Jacques Primois; **136–141** Simon Brown/Conran Octopus; **142–145** World of Interiors/Peter Woloszynski; **146–151** Luc de Champris for Maison Française (Anne Marie Beretta); **152–155** Vogue Living/Rodney Wiedland (architect Ray Gill); **156–163** Camera Press; **164–169** Fritz von der Schulenberg; **170–175** Ianthe Ruthven; **176–181** Vogue Living/Rodney Wiedland; **182–185** Fritz von der Schulenberg; **186–189** Casa Vogue/Giovanna Piemonti; **190** World of Interiors/Clive Frost; **191** courtesy of Powell-Tuck, Connor and Orefelt Ltd; **192–193** World of Interiors/Clive Frost; **194–197** George Mott/Conran Octopus (architect Robert Stern); **198–205** World of Interiors/James Mortimer; **208** Michael Boys; **Endpapers** Trustees of the Victoria and Albert Museum.